Adoption

and

Ethics

A SERIES BY MADELYN FREUNDLICH

THE IMPACT OF ADOPTION ON MEMBERS OF THE TRIAD

CHILD WELFARE LEAGUE OF AMERICA
THE EVAN B. DONALDSON ADOPTION INSTITUTE

The Child Welfare League of America is the nation's oldest and largest membership-based child welfare organization. We are committed to engaging people everywhere in promoting the well-being of children, youth, and their families, and protecting every child from harm.

CHILD WELFARE LEAGUE OF AMERICA, INC.
Headquarters
440 First Street, NW, Third Floor, Washington, DC 20001-2085
E-mail: books@cwla.org

CURRENT PRINTING (last digit)
10 9 8 7 6 5 4 3 2 1

Cover design by James Melvin
Text design by Peggy Porter Tierney

Printed in the United States of America
ISBN # 0–87868-806-4

Library of Congress Cataloging-in-Publication Data
    The impact of adoption on members of the triad /Madelyn Freundlich and Joy Kim Lieberthal.
        p. cm.
    Includes bibliographical references.
    ISBN 0-87868-806-4
    1. Adoption--Psychological aspects. 2. Adopted children--Psychology 3. Adoptees--Psychology. 4. Adoptive parents--Psychology. 5. Birthparents--Psychology. I. Lieberthal, Joy Kim. II. Child Welfare League of America. III. Evan B. Donaldson Adoption Institute. IV. Title.

HV875 .F75 2001
362.73'4'019--dc231

00-052400

Contents

Acknowledgments

The authors acknowledge a number of individuals who provided assistance in the development of this publication on the impact of adoption on members of the triad. The following individuals generously gave of their time and expertise in reviewing drafts and offered critical guidance and suggestions: Dr. Diana Edwards, Professor of Anthropology, Silver City, NM; Lynn C. Franklin, Lynn C. Franklin Associates, Ltd., New York, NY; Joan Hollinger, The University of California at Berkeley School of Law, Berkeley, CA; Deborah Johansen, Deborah Johansen & Associates, Carmel Valley, CA; Margaret Rhodes, University of Massachusetts, Brookline, MA; Brenda Romanchik, R-Squared Press, Royal Oak, MI; Carol Schaefer, New York, NY; and Ann Sullivan, Senior Consultant, Child Welfare League of America, Washington, DC.

The research and editorial assistance of Leigh Nowicki and Premila Reddy, Program Assistants at The Evan B. Donaldson Adoption Institute, is also gratefully acknowledged. Their ongoing support and expertise were essential to the completion of this volume.

Madelyn Freundlich and Joy Kim Lieberthal

Preface

This title is the third in a series of publications developed by the Evan B. Donaldson Adoption Institute and published by CWLA Press. The series is part of the Adoption Institute's multiyear initiative focused on ethical issues in adoption. It is designed to provide the field with a synthesis of the current base of knowledge on key adoption policy and practice issues—issues that currently pose challenges to adoption professionals and which are likely to confront the field in the future. This volume on the impact of adoption on members of the triad follows earlier publications on the role of race, culture, and national origin in adoption and market forces in adoption. The final publication in this series will focus on the cross cutting issues in adoption and the reproductive technologies.

Why a Focus on Ethics in Adoption

Adoption is a complex subject, with social, psychological, legal, and cultural dimensions. It is shaped by policy—at the international, national, state, county, and agency levels—and by practice—on the part of social workers, attorneys, judges, mental health professionals, and others. It involves the needs, interests, and rights of children, birth parents, relatives, foster parents, adoptive parents, and adult adoptees. Adoption includes domestic adoptions of healthy newborns, international adoptions of children from dozens of countries with widely varying policies, and adoptions of children in foster care in this country. Because of this complexity, adoption has been and continues to be the subject of much debate. The controversies in adoption have extended across a spectrum of policy and practice issues, and although the contentious issues have become clear, resolution has not been achieved nor has consensus developed regarding a framework on which to further quality adoption policy and practice.

Productive outcomes have been hindered by the constituency-based considerations that have shaped, to a great extent, the tenor of the debate. Emotion and rhetoric have come to characterize much of the discussion and, as a result, it has been difficult to focus on substantive issues in a reasoned and informed manner or clarify the goals and principles that can assist in resolving the many points of disagreement. From the divisive debates on access to identifying information, to the emotionally-laden controversies on transracial adoption, to the increasingly intense disputes over the competing "rights" of members of the adoption triad—the environment surrounding adoption has become highly charged and focused efforts to craft quality policy and practice more difficult to achieve.

The Adoption Institute, in collaboration with leading thinkers in the field of adoption from across the country, approached this environment by proposing an ethics-based framework for analyzing and resolving the complex challenges in adoption. The decision to utilize an ethics-based approach was based, first, on a belief that ethics could provide a method for reframing the critical issues in adoption and avoiding the divisiveness that has impeded the resolution of the key challenges. Second, the choice of an ethics-based approach was based on an assessment that such a framework would support the identification of the range of issues that impact contemporary adoption, the analysis of relevant considerations from multiple perspectives, and the development of a course of action for improving future policy and practice. The Adoption Institute's ethics initiative has three major components:

- an identification and examination of the core values and principles that underlie quality adoption policy and practice;

- thorough analyses of the critical policy and practice issues that demand attention; and

- the development of a strategy that draws on a sound knowledge base to advance quality adoption policy and practice in the future.

The Critical Issues in Adoption

Because adoption is complex, bringing to the fore many competing interests, values, perspectives, and constituencies, it is not an easy task to reach consensus on which issues represent the most critical questions. The Adoption Institute approached this challenging process by first bringing together a multidisciplinary Ethics Advisory Committee. The members of this group represent a rich diversity of professional backgrounds and expertise, including adoption practice and policy, clinical psychology, sociology, political science, the law, the judiciary, bioethics, medicine, medical anthropology, religion, and social science research. With the guidance of this Committee, the Adoption Institute identified key ethical issues that affect adoption policy and practice and prioritized the most critical issues for in-depth analysis and action. The following topics were selected as critical areas for ongoing attention and work:

The Impact of Adoption on Adopted Persons, Birth Parents, and Adoptive Parents

This topic—the focus of this volume—focuses on the many ways that adoption may impact each member of the adoption triad. For the adopted person, adoption may affect the individual's overall adjustment and well-being, as well as the ability to develop a personal identity. What are the outcomes for adopted persons, and to what extent do past and current adoption practices affect those outcomes? For the birth parent, adoption practice and law may impact, both in the short and long term, an individual's sense of personal integrity. To what extent are birth parents well served by adoption and how do societal perceptions of birth parents affect their sense of well-being? For adoptive parents, adoption involves achieving parenthood in a nontraditional way. To what extent does being "approved" to parent impact adoptive parents? Do adoptive families face special challenges in a society that accords primacy to biological bonds?

The Role of Race, Culture, and National Origin in Adoption

This topic—on which a previous volume focused—considers critical questions regarding the role of race, culture, and national origin in adoption from the perspective of individuals served by adoption and from a broad policy perspective. In this complex area of adoption policy and practice, there are many unresolved questions related to the role of race, culture, and national origin in an adoptee's personal identity and the extent to which racial and cultural similarities and differences between adoptive parents and children should be taken into account. These questions have been placed at the forefront of the policy debate as a result of recent changes in federal law—which now prohibits consideration of race in the adoptive placement of children in foster care; debates related to the Indian Child Welfare Act; and the mandates of the Hague Convention on Intercountry Adoption.

The Market Forces in Adoption

This topic—also the focus of a previous volume—considers various aspects of the "business" of adoption in terms of market factors. With the shifting demographics of infant adoption, international adoption, and special needs adoption, issues are raised about the role of money in adoption, who holds the "power" in adoption, and to whom adoption professionals are accountable. Increasingly, the field of adoption struggles with such questions as: To what extent has there been a commodification of children who are placed with adoptive families? How is the adoption process regulated and by whom? How are the roles of birth and adoptive parents affected by differences in resources? Is the concept of accountability relevant to adoption, and if so, how? Do market forces undermine ethical adoption practice?

Adoption and Assisted Reproduction

This fourth topic raises the question of whether assisted reproduction (including sperm donation, egg donation, and embryo implantation), which may or may not provide a child genetically connected to one or both parents, create a situation that is analogous to adoption. Should the knowledge that has been acquired in the field of adoption be applied in the area of reproductive technologies? Are issues in adoption—such as identity, access to background information, and search—equally applicable in the context of reproductive technology? Should any or all adoption practice standards apply in assisted reproduction?

The Ethics in Adoption Series

Essential to knowledgeable discussion and issue resolution in each of these four areas is a sound understanding of the current knowledge base—the research, the practice-based knowledge, and the policy analyses advanced by leading thinkers in the many fields bearing on adoption: social work, law, psychology, child and adolescent development, medicine, and education. The four publications that form the series are designed to provide a synthesis of the existing knowledge base that can inform and challenge thinking and analysis in each of the critical topic areas. They outline the key issues; review the current data, including statistical information to the extent it exists; identify the research that addresses the key issues; describe the current practice-based knowledge; and synthesize the policy arguments that have been advanced and debated. Whenever possible, the strengths and weaknesses of various perspectives are assessed.

The publications, including this volume which focuses on the impact of adoption on members of the triad, are not designed to take a position on the issues or advance a specific viewpoint as to what is "ethical" or "unethical." It is only through ongoing discussion that consensus can be reached as to what represents the most ethical course of action in adoption—for those directly touched by adoption and for those who provide professional adoption services. It is hoped that the publication series will provide a tool for furthering this discussion—a springboard for advancing adoption policy and practice currently and into the future.

Introduction

Critical to any consideration of the issues that confront the field of adoption today is the impact of adoption on those served through this service—adopted individuals, as children and as adults; birth parents—both birth mothers and birth fathers; prospective adoptive parents; and adoptive families. There are critical questions about the effects of adoption practice and policy on those who are viewed as the "clients" of adoption services. There is considerable complexity surrounding these questions, however, because of a lack of consensus as to who is the client in adoption. Babb [1995] found in her survey research—conducted with child placing licensors for the fifty U.S. states and representatives of professional and child welfare associations, and adoption-related organizations—that there was significant disagreement among professionals regarding who holds client status in the provision of adoption services. Responding from the perspective of infant adoption, some respondents considered the unborn child in a proposed adoption the client; others identified the expectant mother as the client; some said that the mother and the child were the clients; and close to one-half of the respondents (45%) identified the expectant mother, her unborn child, *and* the prospective adoptive parents as the clients. Interestingly, none of the respondents replied to the question from the standpoint of older child adoption, particularly children in foster care who have adoption as their permanency plan, or from the standpoint of international adoption.

The complexity surrounding an understanding of the impact of adoption on triad members also arises from the widely varying views of the purpose of adoption and, even when there is consensus on the purpose of the service, how the underlying purpose is achieved. Dukette [1984, p. 241], for example, writes that "any assessment of value issues in adoption must be made in the context of the only reason for the institution of adoption to exist: providing for the healthy rearing of children." Although this view of adoption has wide acceptance [see Child Welfare League of America 2000], concerns increasingly are expressed that adoption—particularly infant adoption in the United States and international adoption—has been transformed into a service which has, as its core purpose, the finding of healthy babies for adults who wish—and can pay large fees—to adopt [Freundlich 2000b]. Even among those who believe strongly that the purpose of adoption is to provide "for the healthy rearing of children," there is considerable disagreement as to the meaning of that concept. Baran and Pannor [1990], for example, write that "health" for adopted individuals necessarily incorporates a sense of completeness made possible by access to information about their origins. The National Council for Adoption [1997a], however, disagrees, arguing that the healthy rearing of children means the severance of any connection with birth parents and the protection of the integrity of the adoptive family by preventing intrusion by birth families.

It is clear that adoption is fraught with conflicting values and interests [Dukette 1984]. This volume considers the many conflicts from the perspective of each of the members of the adoption triad. After a brief review of the historical context of adoption in the United States, the impact of adoption on adopted persons is examined. Consideration is given to the extent to which the research and clinical literature can provide a better understanding of the psychological and social adjustment of adopted children and adolescents and the challenges they may face; the processes by which adoptees form a sense of personal identify; the role of openness in adoptees' identity formation; and the extent to which access to information and search and reunion play a role in adult adoptee well-being. Second, the impact of adoption on birth parents is considered, with a focus on the effects on birth mothers and birth fathers of the decision to place their children for adoption; the practice and legal issues bearing on their consent to adoption; the special issues involved in situations involving the involuntary termination of parental rights; the impact of international adoption on birth parents in children's countries of origin; and the implications for birth parents of greater openness in adoption. Finally, the impact of adoption on prospective adoptive parents, adoptive parents, and adoptive families is assessed through the lens of social and cultural attitudes about parenting, with particular attention to adoption practice and policy as it supports or fails to support adoptive parenthood and adoptive family formation.

Part I

The Historical Context of Adoption in the United States

Legal recognition and regulation of the process of adoption have varied throughout history, depending on social and cultural values and norms. Historically, adoption has been defined primarily in legal terms as a means by which a child becomes a recognized member of a family to whom she is not related by birth. Less often acknowledged are the psychosocial aspects of the relationships created by adoption—relationships between adoptive parents and adopted children as well as those between adoptive and birth families. As much a social as a legal construct, adoption has played a significant role in the ways that family and family relationships are viewed in any society. From early civilizations' approaches to adoption through current definitions of adoption and kinship relationships, the historical context of adoption provides a framework for understanding the impact of adoption on all members of the triad.

Early References to Adoption

One of the earliest references to adoption is found in the Code of Hammurabi recorded in 2800 B.C. [Cole & Donley 1990]. Among the 282 codes of law, there were at least six that were specific to adoption. One of these focused on the finality of adoption: "If a man adopt(s) a child and to his name as son, and rear him, this grown son cannot be demanded back again" by his birth parents [Martin 1999]. "Adoption into the group, therefore, meant complete severance from one's original family" [Sorosky, Baran, & Pannor 1984, p. 26]. However, the law also acknowledged that adoption could be terminated if the adoptive parent did not properly care for his son: "If a man does not maintain a child that

1

he has adopted as a son and reared with his other children, then his adopted son may return to his (birth) father's house" [Martin 1999]. Cole and Donley [1990, p. 274] note that Hammurabi's Code, like contemporary adoption law, "reveals that members of that culture struggled with issues of risk in adoption." For example, should an adopted child not acknowledge his adoptive parents as his mother and father, thus failing to honor the relationship, he could be subjected to severe corporal punishment. It is interesting to note that the Code only refers to the adoption of sons, suggesting that the laws were created to guarantee paternal lineage.

Other references to adoption appear in Ancient Greek and Roman law. Although relatively uncommon, adoption was primarily for the purpose of continuing the adopter's family through maintaining family name and property or to perpetuate specific religious rituals [Sokoloff 1993; Sorosky, et al. 1984]. In the late 1700s and 1800s, most European countries, with the exception of England, enacted laws to regulate adoption. As with the Code of Hammurabi, these laws attempted to balance and ensure both the finality of adoption and the protection of "natural" parental rights. The Napoleonic Codes, for example, provided that adoption could occur only under specific conditions: the adoptive parent to be "over 50, sterile, at least 15 years older than the adoptee, and have reared the person for at least six years" [Cole & Donley 1990, p. 274].

Adoption in the United States: Colonial Times through the "Orphan Trains"

Although most U.S. laws are derived from British law, those concerning adoption are an exception because British law did not recognize adoption until the twentieth century [Free 1999]. Yet, early practices in caring for dependent children in colonial America—which set the stage for the development of adoption law in the United States—were influenced by English attitudes about family relationships and maintenance of strict social, economic, and political hierarchies [O'Shaughnessy 1994]. As in England, orphaned or otherwise dependent children in colonial America were subject to "putting out," a system that provided a family with children who were seen principally as an economic benefit, serving as domestic help, indentured servants, or apprentices. Poor children and orphans not "hired" into families were placed in almshouses, workhouses where they "received an education to fit them for future usefulness" [Katz 1986, p. 23], or other public institutions. Though some remained in these institutions for extended periods of time, children as young as six or seven often were subsequently "put out." To the extent that any of these children were adopted, the process was private and informal.

By the mid-19th century, pauperism had become epidemic; the number of almshouses and orphanages had grown significantly and the conditions of these institutions had begun to generate considerable public concern. The religious revival movement of the era, accompanied by the development of charitable organizations and private philanthropy, brought greater social awareness of the deplorable state of these institutions. An 1844 report by Dorothea Dix on the conditions of almshouses in New York City triggered public outrage. Her report revealed that large numbers of infants and young children were housed in the company of elderly and mentally ill adults; disease and illness were rampant; and poor parents, many of whom had brought their children to these institutions as a temporary measure, often were forced to surrender their children permanently [Katz 1986]. Her exposé led to systematic attempts to develop new approaches to meet the needs of poor, dependent, and orphaned children.

In the wake of public concerns about almshouses and orphanages, new organizations—including foundling homes, asylums, and other religious charities—were founded to care for children. Many reformers focused on the benefits of asylums, believing that "a few years in an asylum...rendered these children of poverty much more fit for practical life, and purified them to be good members of society" [Cole & Donley 1990, p. 275]. Another alternative to orphanages and almshouses was developed by

Reverend Charles Loring Brace, who established The Children's Aid Society in 1853 to address the growing number of street children in New York City. Brace believed that "a child who applied himself might rise to a higher position in society" and could become a self-sufficient and competent adult if taught proper skills [Langsam 1964, p. 12]. He implemented his philosophy by housing street children, teaching them basic living skills, and paying them to work.

Brace's belief that poor children could become contributing members of society, however, achieved its fullest expression through his refinement of the "putting out" concept into what became known as the "orphan train" movement. Between 1853 and 1890, the Children's Aid Society arranged for trains to transport approximately 90,000 children, ranging in age from 2 to 14 years old, from New York City to the homes of workers and farmers in the Midwest and other rural locations across the country [Langsam 1964; Sokoloff 1993]. Brace believed, based on the "faith" of Society members and the good will of the families taking these children, that these families would provide children with safe and nurturing homes.

Brace's orphan trains and other efforts met with heavy criticism, however, which continued for almost four decades. Critics attacked the "placing-out" of children to rural locations as an advancement of "an anti-urban, anti-immigrant ideology" [Hacsi 1995, p. 163]. Others criticized the absence of safeguards for either children or their birth families, a situation that led some to characterize orphan trains as "reckless" [Carp 1998, p. 12]. Among the problems cited were that many of the children had living birth parents who had not consented to their children's relocation; the families with whom the children were placed were not adequately screened; and there was no follow-up to assess the safety or welfare of children after they were placed with new families [Sokoloff 1993]. As early as 1884, a completed study of one group of children placed in Minnesota stated that "with respect to hasty placements without proper investigation, the Society stood convicted" [Langsam 1964, p. 62]. Others considered the orphan trains to be a new version of child exploitation. Zelizer [1985], for example, maintains that Brace's placing of children in families was based on the economic value or "usefulness" of the children rather than a concern for their well-being. She [1985, p. 172] writes:

> Brace distinguished his plan of free family homes from the traditional indenture arrangement by the absence of a written contract and the retention of legal guardianship by the Society or the natural parents. But free family homes meant only freedom from contract, not from work.

Finally, there were religious objections to the orphan trains. "Biological parents, particularly Roman Catholics, felt that the whole scheme of western emigration was proselytizing since most of the farm families were Protestant" [Cole & Donley 1990, p. 275]. The fierce sense of religious solidarity engendered by the orphan train movement established the basis for future adoption statutes that would require the matching of the religion of adopted children and prospective parents [Cole & Donley 1990, p. 275].

Changing Approaches to Caring for Children in Need

Concerns arising from Brace's child-placing system set the stage for significant changes in child welfare practice. Carp [1998, p. 12] writes that Brace's program was:

> indirectly responsible for initiating a fifty-year welfare reform movement that culminated in the professionalization and bureaucratization of social workers and an expanded state role in regulating adoptions. [The orphan train system] ignited a heated controversy [regarding] the...relative merits of institutionalization versus family homes for homeless children.

This reform movement was based on a view of children as having social, as opposed to economic, value and on public expectations that the families with whom parentless children were placed were appropriate to care for them. By the end of the 19th century, childhood was no longer viewed as "simply a quantitative stage—children as miniature adults—(rather it) became a qualitatively distinct phase in the life course" [Katz 1986, p. 115]. Consistent with this changing view of children, adoption became more of "a search for child love and not child labor" [Zelizer 1985, p. 170]. As children came to be valued as individuals and not as economic resources, families' suitability to adopt became increasingly important, particularly in relation to noneconomic motivations to adopt. Children's homes and other child-placing organizations began to screen prospective adoptive parents and conduct follow-up visits with families after placement to ensure that they properly cared for the children they adopted—that children attended school, went to church, and were "helpful, just as if they had been born in the family" [Zelizer 1985, p. 181].

As societal views of children and adoptive families evolved, adoption became subject to greater regulation. Although the first known case of adoption in America was in 1693—a case in which an adopted son was named in a will and the name of the child formally changed to that of the adoptive parents [Carp 1998], the first adoption legislation was not enacted until 1851 in Massachusetts. The statute was "particularly notable in that, for the first time, the interests of the child were expressly emphasized and the adoption had to be approved by a judge" [Sokoloff 1993, p. 18]. Cole [1985] observes that this statute and other states' laws that followed it defined adoption as a service for children—who, during this era, were primarily older children and not infants. Cole [1985, p. 640] states that adoption, as formally recognized by state laws:

> was not created to solve the stigma and burden of an out-of-wedlock pregnancy. Nor was it intended to ease the pain of infertility by providing children for infertile couples. That...was merely a fortuitous side effect of the primary purpose of adoption: to provide children with nurturant environments in the care of legally recognized parents whose custody, control, responsibilities, and rights were assured.

Adoption in the mid-to-late 1880s served two complementary purposes: it provided children with families to care for them and with financial security, such as through inheritance rights, and it provided families with the economic benefit of children who would contribute through work or as domestic help. During this era, infants generally were not available for adoption nor considered particularly desirable by families seeking to adopt. Infants of unmarried women faced survival risks, particularly if placed in foundling homes where mortality rates were as high as 85% to 90% [Zelizer 1985]. At the same time, infants could be nourished only through breast feeding, a situation that did not change until the invention of milk laboratories and formula in the late 1890s [Sokoloff 1993; Zelizer 1985]. Social attitudes also made the adoption of infants unlikely. The prevailing ideology was that an unwed mother should "atone" for her actions by rearing her child herself and, thereby, achieve "reformation of character" [Cole & Donley 1990, p. 276]. Because social values and the necessities involved in caring for babies made them "unmarketable," infants who could not be cared for by their single mothers often were placed in baby farms [Zelizer 1985, p. 170]. Single or widowed mothers with babies often had little choice.but to pay a surrender fee to these farms which, in return, accepted the babies for boarding. Although the farms promised to find adoptive families for these infants, such placements rarely occurred [Zelizer 1985, p. 174]. Instead, baby farms, which generally provided poor care, became lucrative businesses. Many babies died early and the boarding fees that their mothers had paid exceeded the costs incurred by farms in "caring" for their children [Zelizer 1985].

The Practice of Adoption in the 20th Century

The 20th century brought about numerous changes in adoption. By the late 1920s, adoption began to be pursued for reasons "more sentimental than economic" [Gill in press, p. 2], and as interest in adopting older children who could economically contribute to the family began to decline, there was "an unprecedented demand for children under three, especially infants" [Zelizer 1985, p. 192]. Increasing rates of childlessness among American couples and greater societal pressures on couples to have babies reversed the dynamics that formerly made infants undesirable. "Nineteenth-century mothers had paid baby farmers to accept their unwanted baby, twentieth-century adoptive parents were willing to pay (over $1000) to obtain an infant" [Zelizer 1985, p. 195].

With greater value placed on children for noneconomic reasons, attention turned to the circumstances of poor working children and abused and neglected children. In the early to mid-20th century, child caring agencies developed yet another new approach to caring for vulnerable children—the practice of paying families a fee to board and care for children who could not safely remain with their own families [Hacsi 1995]. Children were "boarded-out" instead of "put out," with payments made directly to families "in an effort to ensure that children would not be valued exclusively for their labor" [Hacsi 1995, p. 170]. This early form of foster care was seen as particularly beneficial for children "who (were) unattractive in appearance or who (had) some slight physical, mental, or moral defect or peculiarity" and who would not likely be adopted [Hacsi 1995, p. 171]. Payment to families, although designed as an incentive to ensure that children were not taken in as servants, nevertheless raised concerns that families were making money by caring for poor children. Hacsi [1995] notes that the debate over the merits of "putting out," which involved no payments to families, and "boarding-out," with direct payments to families, lasted some 50 years, with the "boarding-out" model finally prevailing.

As the practice of foster care developed further, the profile of children in need of such care began to change. Foster care initially responded to the needs of poor children and those who were abused and neglected, but over time it became a service for children in the juvenile court system and children in urban areas whose parents were addicted to drugs [Hacsi 1995]. Poverty, however, remained the common theme [Hacsi 1995], and foster care for poor children gradually supplanted the care of children in institutions. Katz [1986] notes, however, that the question of whether children of poor parents should be removed from their birth families at all was the subject of ongoing debate. This tension was evident in both practice and policy from the early 1900s through the 1930s. As early as 1909, a philosophy of family preservation was embraced as "almost no one defended the disruption of families anymore. Instead, the preservation of the family became a ritual incantation performed by almost every commentator on family issues" [Katz 1986, p. 115]. That philosophy underlay efforts to expand the role of government in supporting families, particularly through financial aid to mothers [Katz 1986]. With the passage of Title IV of the Social Security Act in 1935, the federal government committed resources to support poor children and their families through the Aid to Families with Children (AFC) program. Financial supports to enable poor mothers to remain at home with their children were consistent with the societal sentimentalization of domesticity that marked the early to mid-20th century [Katz 1986; Zelizer 1985].

At the same time, however, foster care services were being expanded for children who were abandoned, orphaned, or who otherwise could not be cared for by their parents. Through amendments to the Social Security Act, federal funding was committed for foster care services, and to a far more limited extent, adoption. Even with federal financial support for these programs, however, foster care was viewed strictly as a temporary service and not as a permanent arrangement for children as had been the case in the 1800s. Placement of children in foster care was made with the hope that they could "someday be returned to their parents" [Hacsi 1995, p. 177]. The science of eugenics, which emerged in the early 1920s, helped to emphasize the importance of heredity and genetics and the ongoing connection of children with their birth families. In this context, adoption was not viewed as an optimal outcome. As Carp [1998, p. 17] notes, the prevailing view was that "though it is better to be adopted than institutionalized, no adoption relation is likely to be as good as the natural one." Child and family serving agencies, consequently, prided themselves on their ability to keep the number of adoptions to a minimum and suggested adoption only when the "natural parents...(could not) be helped or compelled to meet their obligations as parents" [Carp 1998, p. 16].

Following World War II, adoption underwent a critical transformation as more infants became available for adoption and more families sought to adopt newborns. The greater interest in adoption of infants was "crucially shaped by the twin stigmata of infertility and illegitimacy...a social concern for the plight of the illegitimate child and the political pressure of middle-class childless couples" [Wegar 1997, p. 36]. The numbers of babies born out of wedlock after World War II soared, as did the pressures on pregnant women to place their children for adoption. Societal rejection of the unmarried mother left her with little choice but to "choose" adoption for her baby. At the same time, the growing demand for white infants to adopt was triggered by "wartime prosperity, a postwar pronatalist climate of opinion, and medical advances in infertility diagnosis" [Carp 1998, p. 28]. Eugenic-based theories began to be replaced by environmental theories of child development, and even the stigma of illegitimacy was turned "into an asset by suggestions that 'love babies' were particularly attractive and desirable" [Zelizer 1985, p. 194-195].

From the mid-1930s through the early 1970s, the focus on the adoption of infants began to transform the service so that, in the view of some commentators, adoption came to be "not designed for the children, but for the...parents. The agencies sought to provide their customers — adoptive parents — a flawless product" [Gill in press, p. 10]. In an environment that some describe as based on "child as product" [Gill in press, p. 10], the desirable infant had no mental or physical disabilities and, because the demand for adoption came from white childless couples, was also white. Social workers highlighted their ability to clearly distinguish "normal" children, who would thrive in the positive environment provided by adoptive families, from "defectives," whose genetic backgrounds rendered them inappropriate for adoption [Gill in press, p. 9]. In order to make the appropriate determinations, social workers, for example, retained newborns for observation for a period of time to determine whether they were developmentally "normal" and, therefore, "adoptable," subjecting infants to intelligence and other tests to determine their potential. The purported ability to make such assessments of infants allowed social workers to distinguish themselves as adoption professionals with specific expertise [Gill in press].

Social workers also claimed professional expertise in relation to matching the proper children with the proper adoptive parents. Using the biological family model to guide creation of adoptive families, social workers utilized processes to ensure that "parent and child were physically, ethnically, racially, religiously, and intellectually *alike*" [Gill in press, p. 5]. Prospective adoptive parents were assessed as scrupulously as the children placed for adoption and were expected to be "normal" based on birth family standards. Professional adoption agencies, which Gill [in press, p. 17] states perceived themselves to be "guardians of a conventional (white, middle class) definition of family," approved only those prospective adoptive families who shared characteristics of biologically-created families of the time—average age, normal married life, and traditional gender roles—and those who sought to adopt only because of infertility. Some latitude with regard to these characteristics was permitted, but only within narrowly defined parameters. Social workers, for example, were likely to accept a couple in which the wife smoked—seeing the couple as a "famil(y) with individuality and color"—but were not likely to place a child with a family where the wife did not plan to put aside her career upon adoption—viewing that family as "queer or too far off center" [Gill in press, p. 11–15].

Many prospective adoptive parents rejected by agencies or who feared rejection because of the agencies' evaluative standards sought alternative ways to adopt. Beginning in the late 1930s and extending well through the 1950s, perspective adoptive parents found opportunities through unlicensed intermediaries and unregulated "agencies" founded by wealthy women with little or no social work skills or credentials [Carp 1998]. Although most states by this point had enacted laws governing certain aspects of adoption, they generally did not closely regulate the actual placement of children and, as a consequence, "new" adoption professionals appeared on the landscape. Maternity homes for unmarried pregnant women opened their doors, and lawyers and physicians became more prominently involved in adoption, serving as intermediaries between pregnant women and childless couples seeking to adopt. These professionals, in fact, often offered services that were considerably more attractive to both pregnant women and prospective adoptive parents. Unlike adoption agencies, they were less likely to ask intrusive questions or make subjective judgments [Carp 1998].

Adoption and the Law in the 20th Century

A by-product of the social attitudes about illegitimacy that characterized the 1920s through the 1970s was the practice of prominently marking the illegitimate status of a child on the birth certificate. From the perspective of adoption professionals, this practice generated considerable concern because records of all adoptions, including children's birth certificates, were open to the public [Carp 1998]. Cognizant of the social repercussions of illegitimacy and the potential impact on future adoptions, the U.S. Children's Bureau in 1939 recommended that access to adoption records be strictly limited to the adoptive parents, the child at age of majority, and the representatives of the state department involved in the adoption [Carp 1998, p. 42]. By 1948, in response to the Children's Bureau recommendations and other criticisms of the earlier practice, nearly all states had enacted legislation that required that the original birth certificate of a child born outside marriage be replaced with an amended birth certificate when a child was adopted, and that the names of the adopting parents be listed as the child's parents [Carp 1998]. The scope of these laws gradually evolved: they initially mandated that the original birth certificate and the adoption decree be permanently sealed from the "prying eyes of the public" [Carp 1998, p. 54]; subsequently, they sealed other parts of the adoption record from public access;

and finally, in most states, they extended the ban on access to such information to the parties themselves [Freundlich 1997]. These legal developments were justified initially on the basis of protecting the adopted child from the stigma of illegitimacy, but in large part they were also based on desires to protect the privacy of the adoptive family from the public and from birth parents who might intrude on their lives [Freundlich 1997]. Carp [1998, p. 56] observes that by 1949:

> Children's Bureau officials also began to justify keeping birth records secret by invoking the need to protect adoptive parents from possible interference of natural parents. Such a concern reflected a long-standing fear of social workers…(justifying) confidentiality of birth certificates for reasons other than the welfare of the adopted child.

Wegar [1997] likewise maintains that reasons other than the child's interests lay behind these legal developments. She [1997, p. 28] writes that "the implementation of confidentiality in adoption legitimated the occupational niche of professional adoption workers" and further enhanced their position in providing adoption services.

By the mid-1950s, another aspect of adoption had captured public attention—"the burgeoning black market in adoption" which "gave rise to cries for reform" [Cole & Donley 1990, p. 277]. In 1955, Senator Estes Kefauver conducted a Congressional investigation that denounced "baby selling" as a national disgrace and revealed egregious cases of intrastate and interstate trafficking in children, although the exact magnitude of these activities was unclear [Zelizer 1985, p. 199]. At the same time, media attention focused on the practices of adoption agencies, particularly the psychological testing of children and prospective adoptive parents and the labeling of children and parents as eligible or ineligible for adoption [Cole & Donley 1990]. In 1955, in response to criticisms related to agency practice, the Child Welfare League of America convened a National Conference on Adoption, which prompted "a momentum that has gradually led to significant changes in social service casework policy and practice, not the least of which has been a reorientation of the field toward a 'best interests of the child' philosophy" [Cole & Donley 1990, p. 277].

The philosophy of "the best interests of the child" took on particular meaning beginning in the 1970s as increasing numbers of children began to enter foster care, many of whom had "special needs." At this juncture, adoption practice and policy began to view older children and children with disabilities as "adoptable." As Carp [1998, p. 32] notes, the definition of an "adoptable child" expanded to "any child...who needs a family and who can develop in (that family), for whom a family can be found that can accept the child with (the child's) physical or mental capabilities." Policy promoting the adoption of children with "special needs" took the form of the Adoption Assistance and Child Welfare Act of 1980 (P.L. 96-272), which included financial support for families who adopted children with special needs, as well as mandates for more expeditious permanency planning for children in foster care. Immediately following the enactment of P.L. 96-272, there was a decrease in the number of children in foster care, but by the late 1980s poverty and other social factors, particularly parental drug abuse, again fueled a growth in the population of children in foster care [Hacsi 1995]. At the same time, the number of children in foster care who were adopted— though initially increasing after the enactment of P.L. 96-272— stagnated, remaining in the range of 16,000 to 20,000 each year and representing increasingly smaller percentages of children in foster care [Tatara 1993].

In response to these trends, IN 1997 Congress enacted the Adoption and Safe Families Act (P.L. 105-89), which included mandates related to the achievement of more timely permanency for children in foster care through reunification or adoption. The law set time frames for determining a permanency plan for each child in care and required that petitions to terminate parental rights be filed when certain circumstances existed or the child had been in foster care for a certain period of time. It is clear that the law has prompted an increase in the number of finalized adoptions for children in foster care [AFCARS 2000], but its longer-term impact in terms of permanency outcomes for children is yet to be determined.

International Adoption

Coinciding with developments in infant adoption and the adoption of children in foster care in this country has been the growth in international adoption. Historically, international adoption has taken place in the U.S. in four major waves [Altstein & Simon 1991]. The first wave occurred in the late 1940s and early 1950s with the adoption of children who lost their families as a result of civil war in Greece and World War II in Germany. Although a small number of children also were adopted from Japan by U.S. military families, the majority of children were adopted during this period from Europe and were of the same race and often the same culture as their adoptive parents [Sokoloff 1993].

The second wave of international adoptions was precipitated by the Korean War. Initially, Korean children adopted internationally—from the mid-1950s through the early 1970s—were biracial or of mixed race, having Korean mothers and Caucasian military fathers. After the Korean War concluded, international adoptions of Korean children continued, although these adoptees were generally full-Korean. The international adoption of Korean children has continued—though at a lower rate than was the case in the late 1980s and early 1990s—because of five key factors: the growing demand for healthy newborns to adopt; Korea's ongoing relationship with charitable organizations that opened orphanages in Korea in the 1950s; Korea's economic situation; the limited interest in adoption among Korean couples; the perception that international Korean adoptions are successful; and internal challenges within Korea related to establishing domestic interest in adoption [The Evan B. Donaldson Adoption Institute 1999b].

The third wave of children adopted internationally by U.S. families began in the early 1970s with the opening of international adoption programs in cooperation with Latin American countries.

The international adoptions of Latin American children became of greater interest as the number of children available for adoption from Asia began to decline; awareness of the economic conditions in many Latin American countries and the effects on children increased; and it became apparent that international adoptions could be completed in some Latin American countries with relative ease [Pilotti 1985; Altstein & Simon 1991]. Unlike most Asian countries, some Latin American countries have yet to regulate intercountry adoption and have no specific legislation or defined policies in place [Pilotti 1985].

The fourth wave of children adopted internationally was precipitated by the fall of communism in Eastern Europe in the late 1980s, at which time young Caucasian children from Russia and Romania became available for international adoption. Interest in international adoption from Russia and Eastern Europe rapidly grew as media attention focused on the conditions of children in Russian institutions and orphanages [Human Rights Watch 1998] and on the large pool of Caucasian babies in Romania who were available for adoption because of pronatalist policies in that country [Kligman 1992]. Paralleling these developments in Europe were significant policy changes in China in the 1990s that paved the way for the international adoption of Chinese children. With the implementation of the one-child policy in China to limit population growth, a growing number of children, predominantly girls, had come to reside in orphanages, and Chinese authorities began to allow the international adoptions of these children [Johnson, Banghan, & Liyao 1998]. Since the mid-1990s, Russia and China have become the leading countries from which children have been adopted internationally [U.S. Department of State 2000]. Simultaneously, the United States has become the primary receiving country for these children [Bartholet 1993c], with 16,396 children internationally adopted by U.S. families in 1999, a 231% increase since 1990 [U.S. Department of State 2000].

The rapid growth in international adoptions worldwide has raised concerns regarding the "legitimate international movement of children who had been or were being adopted, (with)...no multilateral treaty exist(ing) to protect these children" [Freivalds 1999, p. 8]. In 1993, the Hague Conference and member countries addressed concerns related to the regulation of international adoption through the "Convention on Protection of Children and Co-operation in Respect of Intercountry Adoption." Signed by 51 countries (the United States among them) and ratified or acceded to by 40 countries (including the United States as of October 2000), the Convention attempts to define international standards and safeguards that will both "protect the rights of the adoption triad" and "expedite the placement of children who need adoption" outside their birth countries [Freivalds 1999, p. 1; Hague Conference on Private International Law 2000]. The impact of this effort is yet to be determined.

Conclusion

Cole & Donley [1990, p. 278] observe that "adoption has undergone a number of radical changes in this century, and especially, in the past few decades." Over the last 20 to 30 years, the definition of family has expanded; adoption has come to be viewed as a service for children; the "best interests of the child" has become the guiding practice principle; and the interests of birth parents and adoptive parents have become more clearly defined. At the policy level, there have been significant developments in laws related to more open access to adoption records, federal leadership in promoting permanency for children in foster care, and beginning efforts to regulate intercountry adoption. At the practice level, openness in adoption, planning processes to move children in foster care to permanency in a more timely way, and efforts to develop services for internationally adopted children from diverse cultures pose new questions regarding the impact of adoption. The historical antecedents of adoption provide a basis for considering in greater detail the impact of adoption on adoptees, birth parents, and adoptive parents.

Part II

The Impact of Adoption on the Adopted Person

There are varying perspectives on the impact of adoption on the adopted person. From one perspective, adoption—because it provides a child with the security of a loving and permanent family when the child's birth parents cannot or will not do so—is wholly beneficial for the adopted person. In this view, adoption is the "perfect solution" for children in need of parents, as well as for their adoptive and birth parents [Wegar 1997]. The diametrically opposed perspective is that adoption is almost completely harmful to the adopted person—psychologically, socially, and culturally. As Wegar [1997, p. 2] describes this perspective, adoption is viewed as "an oppressive institution that ignores and contradicts adoptees' real needs and interests." From yet another perspective, the impact of adoption on the adopted person is complex, providing important benefits, but at the same time presenting stresses and challenges.

A consideration of the impact of adoption on the adopted person necessarily focuses on the interrelated issues of adoptees' overall well-being and their ability to develop a full sense of personal identity. These issues are complicated by the many variations in adoption: age at time of adoption, particularly differences between individuals adopted as infants and those adopted at older ages; individuals' preadoption histories; potential differences for individuals adopted domestically and those adopted internationally; composition of the adoptive family, with such variations as racial or cultural similarities or differences among family members and the presence or absence of other adopted or biological children in the home; the extent to which the adoption may be "open" or "closed"; and the family and community environments in which adopted persons are raised. This section addresses the broad issues that have been identified in relation to the impact of adoption on the adopted person, recognizing that there are many individual differences that neither research nor the practice-based literature can adequately address. Focus will be placed on the overall adjustment and well-being of adopted children, adolescents, and adults—as explored in the clinical literature and research; identity formation for adopted persons in general and, more specifically, in relation to open adoption arrangements; and the impact on adult adoptees of policies and practices related to access to identifying information and to search and reunion.

Adoption and Children's and Adolescents' Adjustment and Well-Being

The adjustment and general well-being of adopted children and adolescents have been addressed extensively in the clinical literature and have been the subject of many studies. The clinical literature provides an understanding of the themes believed to characterize the psychosocial functioning of adopted persons in childhood and adolescence. It tends to highlight issues related to adoptees' feelings of loss, although it is clear that the extent to which individual adoptees experience loss varies significantly. The research also provides guidance in understanding the general psychological and developmental impact of adoption on children and adolescents, although a number of questions remain as to the validity and meaningfulness of these findings. The range of findings in the research on the adjustment and well-being of adopted persons, as compared to nonadopted individuals, highlights the complex issues that appear to influence the outcomes for individuals who are adopted.

The Clinical Literature: The Adjustment of Adopted Children and Adolescents

A framework on which researchers and clinicians broadly rely when considering the adjustment of adopted children and adolescents is David Brodzinsky's [1990] stress and coping model. His model is based on two assumptions: first, the adopted child experiences adoption in terms of loss; and second, the adoptee's adjustment to adoption is mediated by cognitive appraisal processes and coping efforts. In this model, background variables— both biological (such as genetic history) and environmental (such as social support and family resources and demands)—influence personal variables such as the adoptee's sense of self-esteem, interpersonal trust, and sense of mastery. This interaction is mediated, however, by the adopted individual's coping efforts and cognitive appraisal abilities. The outcomes for adopted persons, as a result, are associated with both the interactive relationships among biological, environmental, and personal variables, and the nature and strength of the adoptee's ability to cope with and cognitively adapt to the realities of his or her adoption.

The core assumption of Brodzinsky's model, and an assumption that is shared by many other researchers and clinicians, is that loss—and, specifically, loss of birth family—is the experiential basis for adoption. Adoptees are therefore expected to be more poorly adjusted psychologically than nonadopted persons are. Because the model, however, also identifies adoptees' strengths in the form of coping skills and cognitive appraisal processes that mediate the experience of loss and the psychological stress that accompanies it, adequate psychological adjustment is expected for some adoptees. Adopted persons who sufficiently develop and utilize skills in the areas of cognition and coping, as a result, may show a level of psychological adjustment that is only minimally different from that of nonadoptees. This model provides a starting point for a consideration of the adjustment of adopted children and adolescents from a clinical perspective.

Separation and loss and adoptees' perceptions of their "differentness" are frequent themes in the clinical literature on adoption. Nickman [1985], for example, like David Brodzinsky [1990], writes that adoption is inextricably associated with loss at multiple levels. Loss has been conceptualized as a key component in adoptees' developmental understanding of adoption [Brodzinsky et al. 1986]. From this perspective, children placed in infancy slowly experience loss as they mature and begin to understand what adoption involves [Brodzinsky et al. 1998]. Brodzinsky and colleagues [1986] write that by school age, children begin to appreciate the differences between adoption and entering a family through birth, and at that point—realizing that a second set of parents exists for them—they confront the reality of loss and abandonment. Feelings of loss may be accentuated by information they receive about themselves—that they were not planned, could not be cared for, were perhaps unwanted, or were loved but "given away" because it was "best" for them [Rosenberg 1992]. Rosenberg [1992, p. 90] writes that for adoptees, the understanding that they were "given away" for adoption "certifies their being a problem; they are people whose very being caused a problem, one that was solved by extrusion." The effect of this information on adoptees will vary, depending, as Brodzinsky's model suggests, on the individual's coping and cognitive appraisal skills. Rosenberg [1992, p. 121], for example, writes:

> All adoptees struggle with the significance of the fact of their relinquishment. Given differing personalities, some will "think it out," some will "talk it out," some will "act it out," and some will resort to a combination of these approaches.

Ann Sullivan [personal communication, September 16, 1999] notes that an adoptee's coping and cognitive appraisal skills may be enhanced by what may be, particularly for individuals adopted as infants, a number of years of loving and supportive parenting, which provides the adoptee with a sense of self-worth and belonging. Awareness on the part of adoptees that their first families "gave them away" as infants has also been associated clinically with fears of abandonment and worries about the permanency of membership in their adoptive families [Brodzinsky et al. 1995]. David Brodzinsky [1987, 1990] writes that particularly when children have no contact with or no firsthand knowledge of their birth families—as opposed to adoptions in which there is open communication between the child and adoptive family, on the one hand, and the birth family, on the other—feelings of loss and abandonment may be complicated further. The understanding that birth parents are still alive, or are presumed to be, may cause children to worry that their adoptive families may reject and/or abandon them or that their unknown birth parents will return and reclaim them, precipitating the loss of their adoptive families [D. M. Brodzinsky 1987, 1990].

Modell [1994] identifies an additional aspect of the sense of loss and fear of abandonment that children adopted as infants experience—their understanding that they were "chosen" by their adoptive parents. The "chosen child" story, which adoption practitioners have encouraged adoptive parents to share with their children from the post-World War II era to the present, has played a powerful role in the experiences of virtually all adopted children [Modell 1994]. The story portrays the adopted child as a "special" child chosen by parents who truly loved and wanted him, a status that Modell [1994] believes imposes a significant burden on the adopted child. She suggests that when children understand that entry into their families is through selection, they also recognize that they may be "unselected"—that is, rejected or abandoned a second time—particularly if they fail to continue to be or behave as the "special" children that they are told they are. Adding to the fear of being "unchosen" is the very notion of selection itself. Modell asks, "Does a 'picked out' person really belong to his or her parents, especially in a culture that assumes people come inevitably and naturally into the family?" [1994, p. 129]. She found in her interviews with adoptees that the story of being "chosen" undermined their sense of belonging to their adoptive families and "created a tenuous bond, a frail basis for what was supposed to be a nonconditional, enduring relationship" [1994, p. 132].

For children placed at older ages, loss likewise has been viewed clinically as an integral part of the adoption experience, particularly when children's contacts with their birth families are terminated at the time of adoption. An older child may experience loss in an acute and traumatic manner when she is adopted by a new family and all connections with birth family and/or her former caregivers, such as foster parents or relatives, abruptly end [Brodzinsky et al. 1998]. The adoptive placement itself may be undermined by the child's sense of loss of birth family or other significant parenting figures: feelings of loss may compromise the child's ability to accept the adoptive family and cause the child to actively resist the adoption [Borgman 1981]; the child may experience loyalty conflicts which are difficult to resolve [Smith & Howard 1994]; and behavioral problems may exacerbate as children attempt to understand and cope with the changes in their lives brought about by adoption [Smith & Howard 1994]. Some clinicians emphasize older children's feelings of confusion and ambivalence about their lost relationships with birth parents, which may range from very nurturing to highly neglectful or abusive [Brodzinsky et al. 1998]. Others emphasize that "children feel a strong attachment to their birth parents despite the trauma they may have experienced" [Melina & Roszia 1993, p. 330] and, consequently, suffer a significant loss when their relationships with their birth parents, no matter what the quality, are irrevocably terminated.

In addition to the sense of loss associated with separation from birth parents, extended birth family members, and other significant individuals in the adopted child's life, adoptees may experience other losses that impact their sense of security and well-being. In the case of transracial or intercountry adoption, adoptees may experience loss as a result of disconnections from their cultural and racial communities [Brodzinsky et al. 1998]. As outlined in greater detail in the companion volume on the role of race, culture, and national origin in adoption [Freundlich 2000a], children adopted domestically and internationally may face significant issues related to their racial and cultural identity when reared outside of their ethnic communities. Adoptees' sense of loss may extend beyond disconnections with their racial and cultural communities to genetic disconnections. Small [cited in Winkler et al. 1988, p. 85], for example, writes:

> For the child, adoption always means a loss of relationship with emotionally significant objects and a symbolic loss of roots, a sense of genetic identity, and a sense of connectedness. Becoming disconnected from one's ancestry is perhaps the loneliest experience known.

The issue of genetic connections is discussed in greater detail in the following section that focuses on identity issues for adoptees.

The clinical literature also associates adoptees' sense of loss with feelings of rejection and of being "different." Many clinicians posit that a sense of rejection and "differentness" is a powerful dynamic underlying adoptees' adjustment difficulties. Finley [1999, p. 362] observes that "many adoptees experience a lifelong fear of abandonment and rejection along with feelings of being different, of not belonging, and of being powerless over what has happened in their lives." These feelings may be particularly intense for children adopted at older ages from the foster care system whose histories involve significant abuse or neglect. These children may interpret their preadoption experiences as indicative of their lack of worth and essential "badness," and it may be that these experiences with maltreatment are as, if not more, powerful than adoption in contributing to their sense of "differentness" [Sullivan, personal communication September 16, 1999]. Whether flowing from the fact of adoption itself or from preadoption experiences, adoptees' feelings of being "different," rejected, and "bad" are consistently highlighted by clinicians. Anthony [1990, p. iv], for example, writes:

> Added to these basic feelings of being unconnected and different are [adoptees'] feelings of being unwanted and of being unwanted because of 'badness' inside oneself. The theme of being unwanted leads inevitably to thoughts of not belonging and perhaps eventually of not wanting to belong.

Pavao [1998, p. 89], emphasizing the experiences that may underlie adoptees' sense of differentness, writes, "We adopted people were *taken*, and *moved*, and *transplanted*, and given *new* names and *new* identities" (emphasis in original).

Rejection also may play a powerful role in adoptees' lives, whether the decision regarding their adoptive placements was voluntary on the part of their birth parents or the result of the involuntary termination of the birth parents' parental rights. For children whose parents voluntarily placed them for adoption, feelings of rejection may be based on the belief that they were unwanted and "given away" because their birth parents found them undesirable [Brodzinsky et al. 1998]. For children whose parents' rights were involuntarily terminated because of abuse or neglect, feelings of rejection may be associated with an internalization of negative characteristics of their birth parents and a diminished sense of self-worth [Brodzinsky et al. 1998]. In both instances, the sense of rejection may lead to an adoptee's belief that he or she is unacceptably "different" and, by extension, undesirable or unworthy.

Adoptees' perceptions of themselves as different appear to be reinforced by social attitudes and assumptions about adoptees [Brodzinsky et al. 1998]. On a personal level, adopted children may feel stigmatized as a result of the sympathy extended by their friends because they are adopted or because of taunting and ridicule from their peers [Brodzinsky et al. 1998]. Although there have been no systematic studies of the impact of stigmatizing attitudes on adoptees' sense of self [Wegar 1997], the few studies that have addressed the issue suggest that young adoptees are particularly vulnerable to feelings of "differentness" or low self-worth because of negative comments from their peers [Rosenberg & Horner 1991].

Adopted children and adolescents also may be affected by broader societal attitudes that stigmatize adoptees as troubled individuals. Although American culture tends to accord great power to nurture, there is a recurring theme related to the power of nature—that is, the impact of biology and heredity—on personality and behavior [Wegar 1997]. In the context of the influence of biology and heredity on adoptees, societal attitudes may be most strongly rooted in negative perceptions of unwed mothers, which, over time, have "gone from a fallen woman to be saved to sexual delinquent to be controlled to a neurotic girl to be cured" [Kunzel 1993, cited in Wegar 1997, p. 38]. Given such societal beliefs about birth mothers, it is not surprising that general perceptions about the power of biology have given rise to the myth of the "bad seed," an enduring characterization of adoptees that surfaces in a variety of contexts, including entertainment programming and criminal psychology [Hartman & Laird 1990].

There is ample evidence of media portrayals of adoptees as "bad seeds" in television programming and movies [see Waggenspack 1998]. Although this theme in entertainment programs may play some role in shaping public attitudes about adoptees [see Evan B. Donaldson Adoption Institute 1997], the work of individuals such as Kirschner who has theorized an "adopted child syndrome" [Kirschner 1992; Kirschner & Nagel 1988] may contribute more substantially to societal perceptions of adoptees as inherently troubled. According to Kirschner and Nagel [1988], adoptees are at greater risk than nonadoptees for a combination of antisocial behaviors and deviant personality traits that comprise the syndrome—described as including pathological lying, manipulativeness, provocative behavior toward authority figures, and other forms of antisocial behavior. Theorizing that adoptees are unable to integrate two sets of parents—often a "good" set of adoptive parents and a "bad" set of birth parents— Kirschner [1992] has popularized a purportedly scientific view of adoptees that links them with a propensity for criminality.

Although the general public's views about adoptees may be influenced to some degree by such theories, Hartman and Laird [1990] express particular concerns that adoptive parents may be affected at some level by the "bad seed" myth. They note that adoptive parents' "dread of the influence of heredity is often suppressed or denied" [1990, p. 229]. In some cases, anxiety about the impact of the child's genetic heritage may "emerge in an over reactive response to what in other families might be defined as a minor infraction of the rules" [Hartman & Laird 1990, p. 229]. In other situations, though far from the case for all children adopted at an older age [Ann Sullivan, personal communication, September 16, 1999], the "bad seed" myth may lead adoptive parents to fear that the child will not rebound from preadoptive experiences, whether biological or experiential, irrespective of the love and nurture the parents provide [Hartman & Laird 1990]. In cases in which adoptive families are particularly troubled, "the bad seed theme creates a fertile soil for scapegoating, as the family can totally repudiate any connection with the child's problems, attributing all of the family's difficulties to what they have decided are the child's character defects" [Hartman & Laird 1990, p. 230].

As this brief review of the clinical literature suggests, there are a number of themes related to the adjustment of adopted children and adolescents: feelings of loss, a sense of rejection, fears of abandonment, discomfort in having been "chosen," feelings of "differentness," and social stigma associated with adopted status. To what extent do adoptees experience these feelings? Outside of the clinical literature, anecdotal accounts from adoptees themselves suggest that these themes are not necessarily pervasive. While many adoptees state that their adoption experiences incorporate a sense of loss at some level, others focus on their positive perceptions of and experiences with their adoptions, which mediate their sense of loss. For some adoptees, the themes identified in the clinical literature play minimal or virtually no role in their emotional or social lives. When issues related to loss, abandonment, and "not fitting in" do form a part of the experience of adopted children and adolescents, what is the impact on their overall adjustment and well-being? To what extent can research inform an understanding of these issues?

The Research on Adjustment and Well-Being of Adopted Children and Adolescents

The psychological and behavioral adjustment of adopted children and adolescents has been viewed from two different perspectives. The traditional view is that adoption is a highly successful service for children who cannot or will not be raised by their birth parents, and therefore, any challenges associated with loss, rejection, and "differentness" are readily surmountable [Finley 1999]. The other perspective is the epidemiological view that adoptees are more likely to have adjustment problems, as demonstrated by research that shows higher rates of psychopathology among adoptees, and adopted individuals' disproportionate representation among those served in mental health settings [Finley 1999]. The research on psychological and behavioral outcomes for adoptees has produced conflicting results, raising questions about both the traditional and epidemiological views of adoption in relation to its impact on adoptees. The research reporting favorable outcomes has been embraced by those who view adoption as offering positive opportunities for healthy growth and development for children [Ann Sullivan, personal communication, September 16, 1999] as well as those who insist that adoptees are able to achieve a higher level of adjustment and psychological health than they could have reached with their birth families [see Bartholet 1993a]. Similarly, the research showing a higher level of mental health problems among adoptees is relied upon by those who express concerns about the impact of adoption on adopted individuals.

The body of research on the psychological and behavioral adjustment of adoptees is fairly extensive, but the findings may be synthesized into three groups:

- Research findings that suggest that there are no significant differences between adoptees and nonadoptees [Carey et al. 1974; Mikawa & Boston 1968; Norvell & Guy 1977; Plomin & DeFries 1985; Singer et al. 1985; Stein & Hoopes 1985; Thompson & Plomin 1988].

- Research findings that suggest that there are significantly higher rates of maladjustment among adopted individuals as compared to nonadopted persons [Bohman & Von Knorring 1979; Dalby et al. 1982; Dickson et al. 1990; Holden 1991; Lipman et al. 1993; Rogeness et al. 1988; Schechter et al. 1964; Sharma et al. 1996a, 1996b; Silver 1970, 1989; Simon & Senturia 1966; Verhulst et al. 1990a, 1990b; Verhulst & Versluis-den Bieman 1995].

- Research findings that suggest that, on certain variables related to emotional and behavioral adjustment, adopted children and adolescents function at a higher level than do nonadopted individuals [Marguis & Detweiler 1985; Sharma et al. 1996a; Sharma et al. 1998].

Given these conflicting findings, what conclusions about adoptees' adjustment should be drawn? Does the fact that the greater number of studies finds a higher rate of maladjustment among adoptees support the view that adoptees as a group are poorly adjusted? If the findings of higher rates of adjustment problems are relied upon, how should these results be interpreted—as actual psychopathology or as adoptees' efforts to cope with the challenges associated with adoption? And how should these findings be reconciled with findings of equal or, in some cases, better adjustment among adoptees than among nonadoptees?

Three considerations related to the body of research on adoptees' adjustment warrant attention as each has implications when considering the impact of adoption on adoptees: the differences in findings in research with clinical and nonclinical populations; the differences in outcomes for children adopted as infants and those adopted at older ages; and the different comparison groups that are utilized in research and the meaningfulness of the results in relation to those groups [Sharma et al. 1998].

Clinical Versus Nonclinical Populations of Adoptees. Research has focused on adoptees in both clinical and nonclinical settings, and the results vary to some degree accordingly. In studies of clinical populations, adoptees have been consistently found to utilize mental health services at higher rates than nonadoptees. Brodzinsky [1993] has determined that although children adopted by nonrelatives comprise only about 2% of the child population, they make up about 5% of the children seen in outpatient mental health clinics and between 10% and 15% of the children treated in inpatient psychiatric or residential treatment settings. In addition to those studies that have focused on higher utilization of mental health services, other studies suggest higher rates of adjustment difficulties and behavioral problems among adoptees. Studies of clinical populations have suggested that adoptees have higher levels of academic problems [Brodzinsky et al. 1984], acting out behaviors and hyperactivity [Moore & Fombonne 1999; Rosenberg 1992], negative self-esteem [Rohner 1986], and externalizing behaviors [Cadoret 1990]. The research findings related to the outcomes of adoptees in nonclinical settings, by contrast, show differences between adopted and nonadopted persons, but at a far less dramatic level than is evident in clinical settings [Sharma et al. 1998]. One study of adoptees conducted in public schools, for example, revealed that the lower levels of adjustment among adoptees on such factors as drug use, school adjustment, optimism, and antisocial behavior were fairly small when compared to levels of adjustment for nonadoptees [Sharma et al. 1996a].

The differences in the research findings related to outcomes for adoptees in clinical and nonclinical populations raise two questions. The first question centers on the interpretation of the findings of higher rates of mental health and academic problems among adoptees. No consensus appears to exist as to the reasons that adoptees demonstrate higher levels of maladjustment. Brodzinsky and associates [1984] theorize that higher rates of mental health and academic problems among adoptees do not reflect psychopathology but are indicative of the adjustment issues associated with the normal developmental process of adoption. Rosenberg [1992] interprets research findings of higher levels of acting-out and other provocative behaviors as flowing from "an intense need to test the permanency of the adoptive relationship" [1992, p. 76]. Rohner [1986], using phenomenological theory, posits that it is adopted children's perceptions of their adoptions as personal rejections by their birth parents that is associated with adoptees' hostile or aggressive acting out, negative self-esteem, and emotional instability. Cadoret [1990] theorizes a gene-to-behavior pathway for externalizing behaviors and raises the possibility that adoptees may inherit psychopathology from birth parents, a genetic predisposition that then interacts with the adoptive home environment.

The second question centers on the validity of research findings from a methodological perspective. Among the criticisms of research that have been advanced are the absence of comprehensive data on the number of adoptions or the incidence of referrals of adoptees to mental health services on which to base the estimates that appear in the research; the changing characteristics of birth parents, adoptees, and adoptive parents over time, which may undermine the validity of comparisons between different cohorts; and potential biases when researchers are aware that the subjects are adopted [Finley 1999]. Conclusions about the level of adoptees' adjustment problems based on their higher utilization of mental health services also have been criticized. Warren [1992], for example, maintains that overrepresentation of adoptees in clinical settings is associated more powerfully with factors related to adoptive parents than to the nature or frequency of problems among adoptees: adoptive parents' heightened sensitivity to the risks that adoption poses for their children and their greater readiness to seek mental health services for their children; their perceptions of problems associated with adoption as potentially threatening to the integrity of the family and, as a result, their higher motivation to seek treatment; and the higher socioeconomic status of adoptive families that gives them greater access to mental health services.

Infant Versus Older Child Adoption. Studies of adoptees' psychological adjustment have not consistently distinguished outcomes for individuals adopted as infants from outcomes for individuals adopted at older ages [Finley 1999]. A lack of clarity regarding the population of adoptees under study may account, to some degree, for the conflicting findings related to adjustment outcomes for adoptees. Although there are findings to the contrary [see Moore & Fombonne 1999], research generally has supported the belief of many adoption professionals that children adopted at older ages are at greater risk of psychological and behavioral problems [Sharma et al. 1998; Barth & Berry 1988]. Sharma, McGue, and Benson [1996b], for example, found in their multistate study of 4,682 adopted children that, when compared to children adopted as infants, children placed at older ages had greater adjustment difficulties and children placed with adoptive families after the age of 10 years had the most serious problems, including higher rates of substance abuse and antisocial behavior. Other studies have associated older age at the time of adoptive placement with early disruptive life experiences that may affect adopted children's later adjustment. These studies have found that two factors—a history of multiple placements prior to adoption and a history of abuse or neglect—place an adopted child at increased risk for developing adjustment problems [Barth & Berry 1988; McRoy et al. 1988b; Verhulst & Versluis-den Bieman 1992]. Consistent with these findings are research studies that show that children whose adoptive placements terminate before finalization tend to be older at the time of placement than children whose adoptions are permanent and stable [Festinger 1990].

Adoptees as Compared to Nonadoptees in Intact Families and to Children At Risk. A third consideration in the outcome research regarding adoptees' overall adjustment relates to the use of different comparison groups and the meaningfulness of the findings depending on the group with which adoptees are compared. A number of studies compare adoptees to nonadopted persons raised in intact families, and these studies consistently find lower levels of functioning among adoptees [Bohman & Von Knorring 1979; Dalby et al. 1982; Holden 1991; Rogeness et al. 1988; Schechter et al. 1964; Sharma et al. 1996a; Silver 1970, 1989; Simon & Senturia 1966; Verhulst et al. 1990a]. Another body of research compares adoptees to children and adolescents in foster care or institutional settings or to children subject to maltreatment by their birth families, and these studies find that adopted persons function far better [Bohman 1970; Bohman & Sigvardsson 1990; Hodges & Tizard 1989; Triseliotis & Hill 1990].

The findings from the studies have differential applications, an aspect of the research that has not always been acknowledged in discussions of adoptees' adjustment and overall well-being [Sharma et al. 1998]. The research that has compared adoptees to children and adolescents in intact families, on the one hand, has sought a better understanding of how well adopted persons fare as compared to nonadopted persons and, with that focus, has provided a basis for assessing the needs of adoptees and their families and developing responsive services. On the other hand, the research that has compared adoptees to children in foster care or institutional care or in abusive or neglectful birth family environ-ments has sought to evaluate the role of adoption as an alternative for children whose birth families cannot or will not care for them. With that focus, the research has provided a basis for understand-ing the benefits of adoption in relation to nonpermanent, nonfamily and/or compromised family environments. The contributions of each body of research are distinct and provide an understanding of different aspects of adoption in relation to outcomes for adoptees.

A final point bearing on the research on adjustment outcomes for adopted children and adolescents is that, in contrast to studies suggesting that adoptees have higher levels of psychological and behavioral problems, there are studies that find no significant differences in adjustment between adoptees and nonadoptees [Carey et al. 1974; Plomin & DeFries 1985; Stein & Hoopes 1985; Thompson & Plomin 1988]. These findings may be consistent with David Brodzinsky's [1990] coping and stress model, reflecting that the adoptees who participated in these studies had well-devel-oped coping skills and cognitive appraisal processes that medi-ated the psychological stresses assumed to be inherent in the adoption experience.

Less consistent with Brodzinsky's model are recent research findings that adoptees fare better than their nonadopted siblings on certain psychological and behavioral indicators, specifically prosocial behavior, the number of social problems they experi-enced, and the extent of withdrawn behaviors [Sharma et al. 1998]. Because Brodzinsky's model is predicated on loss, there is not an explicit recognition that adoptees could be better adjusted than nonadoptees, and the findings of higher levels of adjustment among adoptees raise relatively unexplored questions about the benefits of adoption for adopted persons. Sharma and colleagues [1998] speculate that their findings of better adjustment on the part of adoptees, particularly in the form of more prosocial behavior, may be attributed to two factors that they view as positive: the adoptive parents of the adoptees may be more inclined toward prosocial behavior and, therefore, provide a role model for such behavior; or adoptees, out of a sense of gratitude, may feel the need to "give back" to the community and, therefore, conduct themselves in a more socially giving manner. Alternatively, they speculate that adoptees may feel fearful of additional loss and behave in prosocial ways in an effort to prove their value and goodness.

As this brief review indicates, the research on adjustment outcomes for adopted children and adolescents offers a range of findings, with some studies suggesting no significant differences between adoptees and nonadoptees; others finding higher rates of maladjustment and utilization of mental health services among adoptees; and yet others noting higher levels of adjustment among adoptees than among nonadoptees on certain psychological and behavioral variables. Interpretation of these diverse findings has been complicated by methodological issues; findings that generalize outcomes for adoptees with very different preadoption histories; and the use of different types of comparison groups in assessing adoptee outcomes. Overall, however, the research appears to suggest that adoptees experience certain psychological stresses related to adoption that may impact their overall adjustment and well-being, although the impact may vary significantly among individuals because of a range of personal, social, and environmental factors.

Adopted Adolescents and Identity Formation

Identity formation, particularly as adoptees move into adolescence and from adolescence to adulthood, is a key issue in the clinical literature [Grotevant 1997; Lifton 1994; Sorosky et al. 1975] and presents a compelling issue related to the impact of adoption on the adopted person. To what extent does the identity development of an adopted adolescent proceed along relatively typical paths or diverge in important ways from identity formation for nonadoptees? Is identity development different for an adopted adolescent compared to an adolescent raised by her birth family? Because of the presumed connection between identity and knowledge about one's background, race and ethnic group, and family history [Phillips 1998], are there unique identity issues for adopted persons? Does the factor of biological origin—which almost inevitably is introduced into adoptive family functioning and which, according to some clinicians, has an important impact on the adoptee's growth and development [Hoopes 1990]—impact on adoptees' identity formation? And finally, what is the impact of openness on a development of a sense of self? The review of the clinical literature and the research on identity formation by adopted adolescents that follows suggests that the answers to these questions are not clear, and that much more needs to be understood.

Adopted Adolescents: The Clinical Literature and the Research on Identity

The development of self, or a clear sense of personal identity, is a pervasive theme in human development literature [Erikson 1968; Marcia 1980; Gilligan 1982]. Despite general agreement that identity is associated with developmental issues of childhood and adolescence, there is little consensus on the meaning of "identity." Schechter and Bertocci [1990], however, note that despite variations in the many definitions of identity, there is general agreement that "identity" incorporates two types of qualities, both of which have significant implications for adopted persons: qualities of sameness, that is, connections with others who are similar to the individual and aspects of the individual that remain consistent, or relatively the same, over time; and qualities of difference, that is, facets of the self that distinguish the individual from others.

Erikson [1959] conceptualizes identity as a continuing process with roots in early stages of development. According to Erikson, the foundation for identity development—the major psychosocial issue during adolescence—is established through resolution of issues in earlier stages of growth: "trust versus mistrust," "autonomy versus doubt," "initiative versus guilt," and "industry versus inferiority." In his framework, the fifth developmental stage, corresponding with adolescence, involves the resolution of the major psychosocial issue, "identity versus role diffusion." Achievement of identity is associated with psychosocial well-being, "a feeling of being at home in one's body, a sense of knowing where one is going, and an inner assuredness of anticipated recognition from those who count" [1959, p. 165]. "Role diffusion," by contrast, is characterized by uncertainties about one's physical self and sexuality, a sense of discontinuity in the self over time, and an inability to make personal decisions, particularly in committing to another person or to a course of action. Erikson [1959] emphasizes that although an individual optimally achieves identity in adolescence, identity formation is the sum of identifications made in early childhood, the psychological facets of the individual's childrearing history, and significant psychosocial events in the individual's life. Consequently, solid family foundations and positive, growth-enhancing relationships with parents are considered critical to the adolescent's successful achievement of a full sense of self [Erikson 1959].

A question on which clinicians and researchers have focused particular attention is the extent to which adoptees' identity formation differs from typical patterns of identity development or presents greater challenges for adopted adolescents than adolescents who are not adopted. A number of clinicians posit that adoptees in adolescence face a more complex task in resolving identity issues than nonadoptees because they confront hurdles related to adoption in addition to issues that parallel those faced by nonadopted adolescents [Brodzinsky 1987; Goebels & Lott 1986; Rosenberg 1992]. Rosenberg [1992, p. 104] writes:

> Achieving the nonadoptee's tasks of developing a separate identity within and establishing appropriate independence from the family is only one piece of the charge for the adoptee. There is an entire other world—of the birth parents and fantasies of them—to process as these adolescents attempt to determine what kind of adult they can or will become.

In addition to the range of complex sexual identification issues which adoptees may confront as they may identify with or react to beliefs about their birth parents [Rosenberg 1992], the process of general ego identity formation may be far more complicated for adoptees. Some clinicians believe that adolescent identity struggles may be intensified by the fact of adoption itself, with early loss exerting significant effects on identity formation [Frisk 1964; Hoopes 1990]. Other clinicians identify specific aspects of adoption that may have a particular impact on identity formation: adoptees' physical dissimilarity to adoptive family members; fantasies about birth parents who are not known to them or not present in their lives; and the need, in some cases, to separate from both adoptive and birth families [Schechter 1960; Sorosky et al. 1975]. Sorosky and colleagues [1975, p. 24] maintain that in relation to identity formation, "adoptees are more vulnerable than the population at large because of the greater likelihood of encountering difficulties in working through the psychosexual, psychosocial and psychohistorical aspects of personality development."

The clinical literature also suggests that adoptees' identity formation may be affected by certain psychological and social factors unique to adoption. Psychologically, the concepts of "family romance" and "genealogical bewilderment" occupy important roles in the literature that addresses identity formation by adoptees, although both concepts are the subject of dispute. "Family romance"—in which it is theorized that children fantasize that they are not the offspring of the average parents who are raising them but, instead, are the children of beautiful and possibly aristocratic parents—is believed to be common among both adopted and nonadopted children during their school years [Rosenberg 1992]. Rosenberg [1992] writes that as children face disappointments in their everyday lives, they are consoled by the fantasy that they have lost their perfect parents and have been shifted somehow to the more mundane parents with whom they are living.

Adopted children likewise entertain this fantasy, but the dynamics of family romance may be more complicated. If, for example, children have been told that their birth parents were too poor, too young, or otherwise unable to care for them, they may be faced with troubling images of birth parents as irresponsible, uncaring, or deficient—images that compete with the image of "perfect" parents that family romance requires [Rosenberg 1992].

As a consequence, the reassuring fantasy of perfect parents may be difficult to develop and, instead, adopted children may have to "deal with disappointments and ambivalence toward two sets of parents" [Rosenberg 1992, p. 100]. Some clinicians suggest that involvement in fantasies about one's "real" family may be more prolonged for adopted individuals than for individuals raised in their birth families [Hoopes 1990], and that adoptees' fantasies about their birth parents may play a particularly powerful role during adoptees' adolescence [Hajal & Rosenberg 1991]. Other clinicians, however, dispute that "family romance" is a universal dynamic among adoptees and contend, instead, that intense or prolonged fantasies about birth parents are specific to adoptees whose relationships with their adoptive parents have been experienced as rejecting [Lawton & Gross 1964].

The concept of "genealogical bewilderment" likewise has been identified in the literature as playing a role in adoptees' ability to establish a positive and complete identity. The term, coined by Sants [1964], refers to an adoptee's confusion and ambivalence when he or she has no knowledge of birth parents or information about birth parents is uncertain. Sants focused on the importance of an individual's sense of genetic and historical continuity, the genealogical confusion that results when such continuity does not exist, and the impact of genealogical lapses on the development of a sense of identity in adolescence. The concept of "genealogical bewilderment" has been utilized to explain the difficulties that adoptees experience in forming an identity when an essential aspect of themselves remains hidden and they have no knowledge of their own genetic identities or of the genetic contributions that they will make to their own children [Frisk 1964; Wieder 1978]. Lifton [1994] refers to this experience of adoptees as "cosmic loneliness"—the sense of alienation that flows from the disconnection from heritage and genealogical roots.

Lieberman [1998, p. 4] takes issue with what he asserts are "imagined but unproved psychological liabilities" associated with adoption. While recognizing that genetic information is germane to health issues, he questions the role of genetic heritage in identity formation and the role of professionals in "fan[ning] the flames of unrest" [1998, p. 3]:

> Professionals ought to reduce unnecessary trauma and risk, yet the history of adoption yields all too many worrisome warnings and anxiety—raising advice by the industry and its experts [1998, p. 4].

Citing the research of the Search Institute [Benson et al. 1994], he argues that adoption is a constructive process rather than one that undermines identity through confusion related to genetic history [1998].

The literature also focuses on social factors associated with adopted adolescents' identity formation and highlights the role that their relationships with their adoptive parents plays in identity development. The quality of parenting, as is the case in all parent-child relationships, has been found to play a significant role in adopted adolescents' identity formation [McWhinnie 1969; Rickarby & Egan 1980; Sabalis & Burch 1980]. Stein and Hoopes [1985], for example, found in their research that adoptees scored higher on ego identity measures when they had positive relationships with their adoptive parents and siblings. Hoopes [1990] has further speculated that positive relationships with the adoptive family may alleviate or eliminate the identity problems that writers such as Frisk [1964] have observed among adopted adolescents.

The literature also indicates that, with few exceptions, adopted adolescents tend to be more secure and have a stronger sense of identity when their adoptive families have encouraged open discussion of adoption [Blum 1976; Schoenberg 1974; Sorosky et al. 1984; Stein & Hoopes 1985]. Although some clinicians point to the dangers of excessive discussion of adoption, which does not take into account the adoptee's individual feelings and needs [McWhinnie 1969], the greater weight of clinical authority supports the benefits of open communication between adoptive parents and their children in relation to adolescents' identity issues. Rosenberg [1992, p. 110], for example, writes that adolescents' separation and search for independence is more positively supported when "adoptees and their parents again look each other over, feel each other out, acknowledge the existence of the birth parents, and reexplore what kind of tie they will have with each other."

Finally, the literature suggests that adoptive parents' attitudes about adoption may play a role in adopted adolescents' identity formation [McWhinnie 1969]. Adolescents may confront greater problems with identity, and, consequently, be at greater risk of developing a negative self-image when adoptive parents feel inadequate about their status as parents [Blum 1976; Brodzinsky et al. 1998; McWhinnie 1969]. Similarly, adopted adolescents have been found to struggle with identity issues when their adoptive parents actively criticize their birth parents [Hoopes 1990]. Adoptive parents' negative views of birth parents may communicate to adoptees a sense of "genetic inferiority" which may not only be associated with socially deviant or delinquent behavior but identity issues as well [Rickarby & Egan 1980].

Identity and the Role of Openness in Adoption

Openness, in which there is some level of continuing contact between adopted children and their birth families, has reached greater acceptance in adoption practice, although not without controversy. Many believe that openness is beneficial to adopted children and adolescents because it meets their identity needs, promotes self-esteem by providing a sense of continuity with their histories, lessens their feelings of powerlessness, allows them to resolve questions about themselves, and assists them in feeling more secure in their adoptive families [Kirk 1985; Grotevant & McRoy 1998; Melina & Roszia 1993; Triseliotis 1993; Ryburn 1995; Silber & Dorner 1990; Gritter 1997]. Others have expressed reservations about openness, including concerns that contact can create divided loyalties for children, jeopardize their secure attachments to their adoptive parents, produce anxieties because children do not have the cognitive capacity to understand the permanence of adoption, and force adoptees to have ongoing relationships with their birth families that they do not wish to have [Kanuik 1994; McWhinnie 1994; Rushton et al. 1993].

Arguing the benefits of closed adoption and pointing out that "there is little evidence to indicate that confidential adoption leads to child pathology," Byrd [1988, p. 22] contends that many elements of open adoption pose risks to children's and adolescents' development and psychological well-being. He describes the benefits of closed adoption for children, although principally in terms of what such confidentiality confers on their adoptive parents. He writes that closed adoptions give adoptive parents "opportunities...to nurture children as their own and in turn to allow those children to internalize a single set of parental values" [1988, p. 22]. He theorizes, without citing research or clinical observations as support, that contact with birth parents detracts from adoptive parents' maximum "attraction to the child without reservation," which in turn interferes with the parent-child relationship and the child's sense of unconditional acceptance and nurturing [1988, p. 23]. Asserting that open adoption presents the same problems as foster care, Byrd [1988, p. 23] writes:

> The potential for negative impact throughout the developmental process appears great. For children, relating to one set of parents is difficult enough. Expecting them to do more than that appears to exact an emotional and psychological toll.

Others criticize greater openness in adoption as communicating a belief in "genetic essentialism," that is, mistakenly attributing overriding importance to genetic heritage in defining identity [Dreyfuss & Nelkin 1992; Carp 1998]. These writers take issue with openness to the extent it suggests the superiority of blood kinship to adoptive relationships [see Carp 1998], a suggestion that they believe undermines the ability of the child to fully identify with the adoptive family.

There is little research on the impact of openness on children adopted as infants because the systematic practice of openness in infant adoption is a recent development, and it is too early to assess the full impact on young adoptees participating in current research [Gross 1993; Berry 1991]. Grotevant and McRoy [1998], based on their longitudinal study of openness in adoption, have reported their initial findings on children's perspectives on their open adoptions—findings that do not appear to support the concerns of Byrd [1988] and others about the effects of openness on children. Grotevant and McRoy found that the majority of children in their study—all of whom were adopted as infants— were curious about their birth parents and birth siblings. Children with less information about their birth parents were more likely to wonder about their birth parents' physical appearance, health, and well-being. Children with more information tended to wonder about what their birth parents had done since they last had contact with them and when they would meet again, or if they had had no contact with their birth parents, whether they would meet. In response to concerns that openness creates a confusing and anxiety-provoking environment for adopted children, the researchers noted:

> It does not appear that providing information about a child's birth parents will confuse the child about the meaning of adoption or lower the child's self-esteem, but neither will it move the child to levels of understanding that are beyond her or his cognitive capabilities to reach. Access to information gives adoptive parents an opportunity to facilitate their child's understanding of adoption [1998, pp. 104-105].

In the clinical literature, Watson [1988] has addressed the concerns expressed by critics of openness, specifically their warnings that children will be confused by two sets of parents and their psychological well-being and identity will be undermined. With regard to the issue of "too many parents," Watson [1988, p. 28] argues that, "It is not openness that gives a child two sets of parents, but adoption itself." He maintains that openness, rather than creating a problem, offers a solution by clearly delineating the roles of the adults in the child's life and promoting honest communication among all affected by the adoption. He also takes issue with the argument that openness undermines the adopted child's or adolescent's ability to form a coherent identity. He maintains that rather than complicating identity formation, openness promotes healthier identity by allowing adopted children and adolescents to integrate their histories and come to terms with the reasons for their adoption. Romanchik [1996] likewise contends that openness promotes a sense of identity, allowing the child to grow up "knowing all the pieces of the puzzle," with access to her history—why she was placed for adoption and the life of her birth parents before the adoption—and to medical and genetic information.

Other clinicians posit that connections with the birth family assist an adopted child to develop a full sense of self by providing him with an accurate understanding of the strengths and weaknesses of his birth family [Rosenberg & Horner 1991; Watson 1994; Littner 1975]. These writers believe that openness promotes the well-being of children adopted as infants because they are not put in a position in which they may exaggerate negative aspects of their birth families and thereby suffer a loss of self-esteem; create romanticized images of their birth parents, which will not be borne out by reality and may deflate the child's sense of self; or see their birth mothers as victimized by the adoption process, fantasize the birth parent's return, and feel anger toward adoptive parents for their roles in the adoption [Brodzinsky et al. 1998; Rosenberg & Horner 1991; Watson 1994]. These benefits of openness were noted by Fanshel and Shinn [1978, p. 489] in an early analysis of ongoing contact between adopted children and their birth families in which they wrote:

> It is better for the child to have to cope with real parents who are obviously flawed in their parental behavior, who bring a mixture of love and rejection, than to reckon with fantasy parents who play an undermining role on the deeper level of the child's unconsciousness.

The research on the impact of openness on older children in foster care who are adopted also suggests certain benefits to children. Research has shown that, in general, children who maintain ongoing contact with their birth parents have a higher sense of well-being and that contact promotes healthy development [Garrison 1983]. The involvement of the birth family and their cooperation with the adoption has also been found to promote the child's ability to accept the adoptive family [Borgman 1981]; resolve the child's loyalty conflicts after the adoption [Smith & Howard 1994]; and minimize negative behavioral responses to the changes brought about by adoption [Smith & Howard 1994]. There appear to be situations, however, in which ongoing contact between birth parents and their children may not be appropriate for children in foster care who are adopted. Appell [1996] suggests that these situations include cases in which there have been multiple unsuccessful placements of the child and the presence of the birth parents presents a risk of future disruption; there is a history of severe child abuse within the birth family; birth parents, as a result of mental health, substance abuse, or other problems, are likely to be unduly disruptive to the adoption; and birth parents continue to present a risk of severe and imminent harm to the child. Even in these situations, however, the literature suggests that contact with other members of the birth family may be beneficial to an older child who has established positive relationships with extended family members [Melina & Roszia 1993; Silverstein & Roszia 1999].

Recent research by Grotevant and colleagues [1999] suggests that outcomes for children in open adoptions may be dependent on a range of factors. These factors may include the parenting style of the adoptive parents (including factors such as responsiveness to the child, warmth and sensitivity, and family structure), the psychological stability of the birth mother, and the social skills of all the adults in the adoptive family network. The researchers also note the potential role of collaboration in the relationships between members of adoptive and birth families in influencing outcomes for adoptees. Defining collaboration as "proactive behavior at the level of the family system driven by a valuing of engagement in the network on behalf of the child" [1999, p. 245], the researchers studied patterns among adoptive families of children determined to be at highest risk for socioemotional problems. They found that the level of collaboration in these families was variable and did not depend on whether the adoption was mediated—that is, an intermediary facilitated the communication—or fully disclosed—in which direct personal contact between birth and adoptive families was made.

The researchers found that adoptive families at the low end of collaboration tended to emphasize problems in their relationships with birth families, were unclear as to how to interpret communication from birth family members and believed that their children should have information, not because of its intrinsic value, but to protect their children from learning about their adoption from someone else. Adoptive and birth families in the moderate range of collaboration were attempting to make the relationships work and to take some risks with one another, but encountered various challenges, including objections from the current husbands of the birth mothers and complexities related to the adoptions of siblings in closed adoption arrangements. Finally, adoptive and birth families at the higher end of collaboration tended to have high levels of mutual respect, caring, and affection, and a commitment to making the relationships work because of their belief that openness was in their child's best interests. Although they noted that more research is needed, Grotevant and associates hypothesized that the level of collaboration among the adults may be predictive of outcomes for children in adolescence when they may begin to manage their own relationships with both their adoptive and birth families.

As this brief review indicates, identity formation for adopted adolescents is a complex issue. The clinical literature and research suggest that achievement of identity may be a more complicated process for adoptees than for nonadoptees, but a range of psychological and social factors appear to affect the process of identity formation, suggesting a variety of outcomes for adopted persons. The research is only beginning to consider the impact of openness on adoptees' ability to form a complete and positive identity. The clinical literature reflects an ongoing debate on this issue. The role of openness in supporting identity formation will be an issue for further study as children whose adoptions are open at the inception enter adolescence and adulthood.

Adult Adoptees' Access to Information and Search and Reunion

The issue of whether adoptees need, for purposes of optimal well-being and a sense of identity, information about their backgrounds and contact with their birth parents and members of their birth families, including siblings and extended family, has generated great controversy [Baran et al. 1976; National Committee for Adoption 1989; Wegar 1997]. To what extent does a relationship exist between adoptees' ability to obtain information about their birth parents and the development of a positive and complete sense of self? Do barriers to information, in and of themselves, affect adoptees' sense of well-being? What is the impact of current constraints on access to information on adult adoptees? And what role do search and reunion play in adult adoptees' sense of well-being? The following review of the literature and extremely limited research in the areas of information access and search and reunion suggests wide differences of opinion on these issues. There is a growing consensus, however, that greater sharing of information is in the interests of adopted persons and that an adoptee's desire to search, when such is the case, should be supported.

Adult Adoptees' Access to Information and Identity Issues

There are significantly different views on the extent to which adult adoptees have cognizable psychological needs for information about their origins. One school of thought holds that information about birth family is not critical to adoptees' sense of personal identity. Lieberman [1998, p. 3], for example, writes that "identity hinges on actual relationships more than on pedigree and genes." He maintains that expert advice related to adoptees' connections with their birth family history, which he describes as "vary[ing] from helpful to useless or worse," may actually disrupt identity formation "in the service of nothing more than a pat formula about what is 'normal'" [1998, p. 3]. He rejects clinical theory that associates adoptees' ability to form a strong personal identity with issues related to the trauma of "being given up;" feelings of loss and rejection that accompany a developmental understanding of adoption; or a desire to know the identity of one's birth parents [1998, p. 3]. Professor Joan H. Hollinger [personal communication, March 30, 2000] in a similar vein, has noted that the development of identity is an extremely complex process and does not turn on single factors such as knowing or not knowing the details regarding one's origins or having an ongoing relationship with biogenetic parents.

The other school of thought is that the ability to obtain information about one's origins is critical to a sense of identity [Arndt 1986; Frisk 1964; Wieder 1978]. Triseliotis [1984, p. 118], for example, has concluded that:

> There is a psychosocial need in all people, manifest principally in those who grow up away from their original families, to know about their background, their genealogy and their personal history if they are to grow up feeling complete and whole.

Many clinicians—including Schechter and Bertocci [1990], Brodzinsky and associates [1998], and Hartman and Laird [1990]—maintain that when adoptees are severed from information about their pasts, they lack the understanding necessary to fully consolidate identity. Modell [1994, p. 135] found in her interviews with adoptees a pervasive sense of being "cut off from a past" and experiences of isolation and emptiness when information about their biological backgrounds was not available to them. She concluded that "discovery of origins, then, is crucial to establishing a sense of identity—and not just any origins, but specifically a biological ancestry" [1994, p. 138]. Similarly, in an earlier work, Kornitzer [1971, cited in Pugh & Schofield 1999, p. 8] wrote:

> Background knowledge of one's family is like baby food— it is literally fed to a person as a part of the normal nourishment that builds up his mental and emotional structure and helps the person to become acquainted with what he is so that he can seize his inheritance for himself.

The relevance of access to background information to adult adoptees has not been the subject of research to any great extent. In a recent small-scale study, however, Pugh and Schofield [1999] reported on the experiences of individuals who sought and received background information about themselves from an English adoption and foster care agency. They observed that "whatever the nature of the information which people uncovered, it almost always generated powerful emotions in them," ranging from excitement and catharsis to pain and anger, particularly when they discovered too late that a birth family member had recently died [1999, pp. 13-14]. They found that despite the initial shock that some individuals felt, there was a consistent sentiment that "even unpalatable information was preferable to living with ignorance" [1999, p. 14].

In the context of these differing views of adoptees' psychological needs in relation to information about their backgrounds, issues have emerged in two key areas. First is the policy arena where the controversy centers on the extent of a "need to know" in relation to legal access to identifying information and, to a lesser extent, to nonidentifying information. Second is the societal arena in which the status of an adult adoptee is defined and the extent to which perceptions of adopted persons have played a role in shaping adoption policy and practice.

The Controversy Regarding the "Need to Know." In the United States, where the controversy regarding access to identifying information continues to rage, the relationship between information about an adoptee's own origins and identity formation remains the subject of debate. Access to birth family information—particularly identifying information but, to some extent, nonidentifying information—is limited, and the ability of many adoptees to obtain a complete preadoption history is constrained by state laws, administrative and social factors, and agency policy. Brodzinsky and colleagues [1998, p. 104] note that adoptees may feel "cut off from much of the information about their origins" because of an inability to gain access to information as a result of a host of barriers that may be posed by adoption agencies, the court and legal system, and by some, though by no means all, adoptive parents.

The controversy about adult adoptees' access to information about themselves—and identifying information about their birth parents, in particular—exists within a broader environment that, since mid-century, has viewed the sharing of background information with adoptees as unwise or affirmatively harmful. Since World War II, secrecy and closed proceedings have marked adoption [Carp 1998]. Social work practice, beginning in the 1950s, limited disclosure of nonidentifying information to both adoptive parents and adoptees in the belief that communicating only selected, largely positive background information supported a healthier adoptive family [Freundlich & Peterson 1998]. That practice has undergone significant change over the past decade and nonidentifying information is now made more broadly available, although there are notable exceptions involving cases in which correct and/or complete information is not communicated [Freundlich & Peterson 1998].

For many adoptees, however, extensive and/or accurate information about their origins is not available. Although some adoptive families provide their children with the nonidentifying information they have about their children's birth families, Partridge [1991] notes that the desire for normality in adoptive families is so strong that some adoptive families push the birth family into the background so that they are not discussed at all. Other clinicians note that adoptees may participate in this process, recognizing that their adoptive parents are troubled by their birth families and that the safer course is to avoid mention of birth parents altogether [Freeman & Freund 1998]. Even when families readily share the information they have with their adopted children, adoptees may find that this information is incomplete or inaccurate. Schechter and Bertocci [1990] describe the experiences of many adoptees who learn from their adoptive parents early in life that they have a different family of origin; find as school-age children that their adoptive parents have little or no specific information about their birth parents—such as who they were, where they are, and why they made the decision to place them for adoption; and then discover as adolescents or adults that the information that the adoption agencies have in their files is significantly different from the information that their adoptive parents received and then shared with them.

Access to identifying information is generally even more elusive than access to nonidentifying information. Beginning in the 1930s, the laws of most states sealed all adoption records, preventing all members of the adoption triad, including adult adoptees, from obtaining identifying information about their birth families. Included in these sealed records were adoptees' original birth certificates [Carp 1998]. The sealing of records was grounded on the belief that keeping the names and whereabouts of birth and adoptive parents "confidential" ensured the integrity of the adoptive family, prevented birth parents from attempting to reclaim their children, and assisted birth parents to "recover" from their "indiscretions" [Carp 1998, pp. 105-106]. The laws in most states—with the current exceptions of Kansas, Alaska, Oregon, and Alabama, which allow adult adoptees unconditional access to original birth certificates, and Tennessee, which allows adult adoptees access to portions of their adoption records—continue to prohibit the release of identifying information about birth parents to adoptive parents or to adoptees even after they reach adulthood [see Carp 1998].

Schechter and Bertocci [1990, pp. 62-63] write that the barriers to information in adoptees' preadoptive histories—particularly the identities of their birth parents—form "a nearly impenetrable iron curtain" that thwarts adoptees' attempts "to establish a full personal history in a way that is unknown in any other psychosocial context." Efforts to remove legal barriers to this information began in the 1970s but were not successful [see *ALMA v. Mellon* 1979]. More recent efforts to repeal sealed records laws through legislative action or statewide referenda have met with judicial challenges, and although the outcomes of efforts to change sealed record laws may be, to some degree, uncertain, the recent decisions of the Tennessee and Oregon Supreme Courts upholding a statute (in the case of Tennessee) and a statewide initiative (in the case of Oregon) allowing adult adoptees access to their adoption records [*Doe v. Sunquist* 1999; *Jane Does, 1, 2, 3, 4 v. the State of Oregon, John A. Kitzhaber, and Edward Johnson* 1999] may suggest a shift in the policy environment.

Some legal scholars have argued that, notwithstanding opposition to opening adoption records, there is a strong connection between identity and liberty interests [Cahn & Singer, in press; Woodhouse 1994], which supports the opening of adoption records to adult adoptees. Cahn and Singer, for example, cite the United States Supreme Court in *Roberts v. United States Jaycees* [1984] in which the Court wrote that the Constitution's protection of close personal relationships:

> reflects the realization that individuals draw much of their emotional enrichment from close ties with others. Protecting these relationships from unwarranted state interference therefore safeguards the ability to independently define one's identity that is central to any concept of liberty [1984, p. 619].

Emphasizing the fluidity of identity, particularly as it evolves over time, Cahn and Singer [in press] argue that the identity interests of adoptees become predominant in adulthood:

> As an adopted child matures...and the birth parent's relinquishment recedes in time, the child's identity needs begin to predominate. By the time a child reaches the age of majority, the child's need to construct her own identity may include the need to know her birth parents. At this point, the child's identity interests outweigh the birth parent's earlier desire to prevent the establishment of a parent-child relationship.

This interest, they maintain, supports adoptees' legal ability to access their original birth certificates, a position disputed by the National Council for Adoption [NCFA], which places primary emphasis on the "personal dignity and autonomy" interests of birth parents and the familial interests of adoptive parents [National Council for Adoption 1997b].

NCFA's position, however, that adoptive and birth parents and adult adoptees have competing interests is undermined by recent data that suggests that all members of the triad recognize the importance of adult adoptees' access to identifying information. Avery [1998] found in her survey of 1200 adoptive parents that 84% of all adoptive mothers and 73% of adoptive fathers supported adult adoptees' ability to obtain their original birth certificates. Studies by Sachdev [1991] and the Maine Task Force on Adoption [1989] found that the great majority of birth parents support adult adoptees' access to information on their birth families. These studies seem to support the conclusion of Cahn and Singer [in press] that:

> Members of the adoption triangle have always struggled with reconciling the (non)existence of their families. Allowing adoptees access to their birth records serves to recognize the difficulties that they experience as they develop their identity, and helps biological parents reconcile themselves to the relinquishment decision. Ironically, without needing to keep secrets, adoptive families may indeed become more like nonadoptive families.

The Status of the Adult Adoptee and Access to Information. An issue related closely to policy questions regarding access to information for adult adoptees is their respective status in relation to other members of the triad. The pervasive conceptualization of the adopted person is not that of an adult but that of an "adopted child" whose interests are assessed in relation to the interests of birth parents and adoptive parents [Kirk 1985; Rosenberg 1992]. This phenomenon may be attributable, at least in part, to the role that the concept of "needs of the child" has played as the guiding practice principle for adoption professionals [Kirk 1985, p. 121]. Although this focus has played an important role in maintaining a view of adoption as a service for children in need of families as opposed to a service for adults who desire to parent a child, Kirk [1985, pp. 120-121] points out that this emphasis has caused professionals to overlook a key reality—the institution of adoption "has never clarified at which point in life an 'adopted child' becomes legally an adult who also happens to be somebody's child by adoption." Jean Paton [1954, p. 5], similarly, has noted that because of a "tendency to be babyish in talking about adoption," little attention has been given to the concerns of adult adoptees.

The lack of attention to adult adoptees and, as a result, the lack of emphasis on their interests, may also be related to the absence of any role for the adoptee in the adoptive placement process. Hartman and Laird [1990, p. 228] argue that adoptees are the most disempowered members of the triad, "having generally had no opportunity to participate in the decisions that have so powerfully shaped their lives and their identities" [1990, p. 228]. The absence of power has been viewed by some clinicians as extending from adoptees' early life experiences into their adulthoods [see Lifton 1994; Sorosky et al. 1984]. The transition to adulthood and adoptees' acceptance of responsibility for themselves, spouses, children, and their own parents is, according to Rosenberg [1992], complicated by societal views of adoptees as "adopted children."

The interests of adult adoptees—particularly in relation to access to information about their origins—have been recognized to some extent by the legal system, but these interests generally have been found to be less compelling than the interests of birth and adoptive parents who may be viewed as the "real" adults with "real" interests. Arndt [1986, p. 119] comments that, "the real, present needs of the adopted person [for his or her background information] are 'balanced' against the theoretical needs of the natural parents" but, typically, the needs of adoptees have been found to hold less weight. Likewise, the interests of adoptive parents, principally framed in terms of the autonomy and integrity of the adoptive family, generally have been balanced against adoptee interests even after adoptees reach adulthood [see Hollinger 1999a]. In the process of such balancing, the interests of adoptees generally have not been found as compelling as the interests in preserving the integrity of the institution of adoption and generally have been required to yield to what have been viewed as the superior rights of both sets of parents to privacy [see *ALMA v. Mellon* 1979].

This view of adoptees has been challenged by a number of writers. Schechter and Bertocci [1990, p. 63] argue that assumptions of superior rights on the part of birth and adoptive parents operate out of a "best-interest-of-the-parent" philosophy rather than a commitment to the "best interest" of the adoptee. The determination that adult adoptees do not have an overriding interest in access to their background information suggests to these authors [1990] that the adult adoptee is essentially being cast as a child whose interests must always defer to the greater interests of birth and adoptive parents. Similarly, Sorosky, Baran and Pannor [1984, p. 122] describe the "perennial child role" that adoptees are required to play as others shield them from information about their origins and adoptive parents are given the authority to determine whether adult adoptees may obtain personal information. Kirk, noting that there is "considerable question" about the benefits of adoption for adoptees *"as adults"* [1985, p. 123 (emphasis in original)], writes:

> But if [adoption] agencies considered the needs of the parents to be secondary to the interests of the children, why were the professionals not able to see that children, including adopted ones, must be allowed to grow up and make adult choices if they are to become full adult members of society? When a person cannot legally obtain basic documents relating to his or her own life, then that person does not have the basic rights and duties of adults as that term is defined in society [1985, p. 121].

The view of the adoptee as an "adopted child" irrespective of age or maturity has historically shaped policy and practice in relation to information access and other aspects of adoption. The issue remains as to the extent to which societal and professional perceptions of adult adoptees have shifted to any meaningful extent and whether their interests can, at any point, enjoy equal, if not greater, weight as those of birth and adoptive parents.

Search and Reunion

There has been much debate about both the degree to which adoptees may search for members of their birth families and the role of search and reunion in the development and confirmation of an adoptee's sense of self [Lifton 1994; National Committee for Adoption 1989; Wegar 1997]. There is no definitive data on the number of adoptees who undertake a search or wish to search for their biological relatives [Wegar 1997], although proponents of the closed record system maintain that "very few adoptees and birth parents seek to meet each other" [National Committee for Adoption 1989, p. 5] and search activists insist that "most adoptees, either as children or adults, would like to meet their birth parents" [Auth & Zaret 1986, p. 567].

The literature suggests that the decision to search is one that adoptees make only after considerable thought. Triseliotis [1973, p. 92] found in his research with adoptees that:

> The step of enquiring and searching was not taken lightly by most adoptees. The final step usually came at the end of a fair amount of deliberation and usually at a stage when it could not be put off any longer.

Research has suggested that adoptees who choose to search may feel embarrassed or guilty about their decision or fearful that others will consider them obsessed or abnormal [Haines & Timms 1985; Walby & Symons 1990]. Modell [1994, p. 150] found in her interviews with adoptees that the decision to search was made "cautiously, aware of the risks in breaking the rules and violating conventions." Many adoptees whom she interviewed reported that they felt pressure not to search:

> Adoptees...heard they were crazy, neurotic, ungrateful for initiating their quest—and, like the unknown birth parents, irresponsible and impulsive. For some adoptees, it was a no win game: 'feeling like we've done something wrong and that we're criminals for having just been born' [1994, p. 150].

She observed that many adoptees continued their searches despite opposition—which for some may have come from their adoptive parents but for many others from the broader social environment—because they felt that "somebody else" had made all of the important decisions in their lives [1994, p. 151]. "Being defined as less than adult and not in control of one's own life course was not unique to searching adoptees, but it was certainly part of their experience" [Modell 1994, p. 151].

There is little definitive information in the research as to adoptees' motivations for search. Research has provided conflicting findings regarding the extent to which adoptees' interest in search is connected to the quality of their relationships with their adoptive parents. Triseliotis [1973] found that search was associated with high levels of dissatisfaction with the adoption experience; other studies have indicated that most adoptees who search are quite satisfied with their adoptions [Day & Leeding 1980]; and yet other studies have found more or less equal distributions of satisfaction and dissatisfaction among adoptees who search [Schechter & Bertocci 1990; Kowal & Schilling 1985]. Research also offers conflicting findings on the relationship between adoptees' fantasies of their birth parents and interest in searching. Schechter & Bertocci [1990], for example, found that searchers were more likely to have positive images of their birth parents, and Triseliotis [1973] found that searchers were likely to hold negative views. A few studies have explored other possible motivations for search and suggested that searching may be associated with adoptees' perceptions that they were markedly different in physical appearance [Stein & Hoopes 1985] or in personality [Schechter & Bertocci 1990] from their adoptive parents and, thus, were motivated by a desire to find family members who physically or temperamentally resembled themselves.

Several clinicians have theorized that one of the key reasons that adoptees search is to consolidate identity. Schechter and Bertocci [1990, p. 80], for example, point to statements on the part of searching adoptees that they have the desire to "find out who I really am," "learn my true identity," and find "the part of me that is missing" [Schechter & Bertocci 1990, p. 80]. They [1990, p. 80] write that:

> Identity does not have closure in adolescence or young adulthood but continues to evolve over the life span and through the search, adoptees are seeking a reconciliation and cohesion of many complex perceptions, cognitive systems, and self-object representations.

Sorosky, Baran, and Pannor [1975] similarly posit that search is linked with identity issues, though they emphasize that search should not be viewed as pathological in nature but as the inevitable outcome of the separation from birth parents. Also addressing the connection between search and identity, Reitz and Watson [1992, p. 237] outline as the major reasons for adoptees' decisions to search:

> (1) the need to know why they were abandoned to adoption; (2) the unique genetic tie to their birth mothers and their need for continuity with their own history; and (3) the need to bring together the disparate pieces of their backgrounds in order to feel that they are whole and worthwhile beings.

Similarly, Campbell, Silverman, and Patti [1991] state that adoptees who search are motivated by four main factors: a life cycle change, such as having a first child; a desire for personal information; the hope that a relationship might be forged with the birth parent; and a desire for greater self-understanding. These researchers note:

> Adoptees who search seem to be looking for ways to build an extended nuclear family, not to replace their adopted family. They seem to need to bring the two parts of themselves together so that they can build a sense of self that feels complete to them [1991, p. 334].

As limited as the information is about adoptees who search and their search experiences, even less is known about adoptees who do not choose to search. The few studies that have compared nonsearchers to searchers suggest that nonsearchers tend to be more satisfied with the level of their adoptive parents' communications with them about their adoptions [Aumend & Barrett 1984]; score higher on scales measuring self-esteem and self-concept [Sobol & Cardiff 1983]; and score lower on scales measuring self-abasement [Reynolds et al. 1976]. The research provides little information on the reasons that adoptees choose not to search when they have information regarding their birth parents. Clinicians, however, have offered several possible explanations, including adoptees' fear of not being able to fully integrate the information they might receive [Frisk 1964]; a greater interest in medical and genealogical information than in actual contact with birth family members [Blum 1976]; and a desire to avoid having information about themselves made available to their birth parents [McWhinnie 1969]. Rosenberg [1992] notes that some adoptees who do not wish to search may feel angry and rejected by their birth parents; others may feel quite satisfied with their lives and do not believe that they would significantly benefit from a search; and yet others may feel anxious about the prospect of a second set of parents in their lives who may introduce additional stresses or complications.

Lifton [1988, p. 81] writes that in failing to search, an adoptee remains a child forever. She maintains that nonsearchers fail to address the fundamental need to connect with their "own kind":

> Nonsearchers, for all their sense of righteousness and loyalty, have always seemed to me self-denigrating . . . There is the implication that they don't have a right to rock their own boat, to pen their own can of worms. They seem to accept that they don't have a right to their own heritage. We see such internalized guilt in them that, even if their adoptive parents should sanction a search, it would be hard for them to follow through. It is as if they have a will not to know [1988, p. 75].

Wegar [1997, p. 131] takes issue with this position, noting that "references to the importance of choice in the search literature mean little if the lack of a desire to search is interpreted as a symptom of negative character traits or individual pathology."

She argues that the understanding of search is partial at best because most adoption research has focused on adoptees who search. She cautions:

> Adoptees, of course, have a variety of needs, and the need to know is not necessarily the same as the need to search...The complex and ambivalent nature of adoptees' experiences has...often been misunderstood. Although it makes sense to distinguish between negative and positive opinions about searching, the tendency to dichotomize [that is, treating searchers and non-searchers as fundamentally different in their psychological make up and adoption experiences] hides the interplay of motives that influence the choice [1997, pp. 66-67].

Summary

The research and literature that addresses the impact of adoption on adoptees offers a range of perspectives. Much of the research points to highly positive overall outcomes for children who are adopted; the research reports less uniformly positive outcomes for adopted adolescents. The clinical literature suggests a number of themes that may arise in the psychosocial development of adopted persons, including loss, abandonment and rejection, "differentness," and social stigmas related to adoption, although anecdotal accounts outside the clinical literature suggest that these feelings and experiences are not necessarily pervasive. The research and clinical literature on adopted adolescents' identity formation suggests that the process may be more complicated for adoptees than nonadoptees, although a range of personal and social factors appear to influence the process. The impact of openness on adoptees' identity formation remains to be determined as the practice has been in place only a short period of time, and longitudinal research has not yet yielded information on the effects of openness on adopted persons. Current research does suggest, however, that adopted children's adjustment is not adversely affected by open adoption arrangements and may, in fact, be enhanced.

With regard to the impact of adoption on adult adoptees, the tendency to regard adoptees as "perennial children" may have a significant impact on adoptees' sense of well-being and complete sense of self. Much attention has been given to the barriers that adult adoptees confront in attempting to access identifying information and to search for and contact birth family members. There is, however, considerable variation in adult adoptees' views of search and reunion, reflecting, as is the case with the range of other adoption issues, varying needs, interests, and concerns among this extremely diverse population of individuals.

Part III

The Impact of Adoption on Birth Parents

From an ethical perspective, an assessment of the impact of adoption on birth parents necessarily involves a range of issues. These considerations bear on the extent to which adoption practice and policy evidence respect for birth mothers and birth fathers; acknowledge the integrity of birth parents as they make plans for their children or as decisions are made to terminate their rights to their children on an involuntary basis; and respond to birth parents' interests in information both prior to and after they have made adoption plans. Issues affecting birth mothers and birth fathers are set within a social and cultural environment that, despite the high value that society generally places on biological connections and the protection of the parent-child relationship [Kirk 1984], has typically cast birth parents in a less than favorable light [Lowe 1999].

This section addresses issues that affect both prospective birth parents (individuals considering adoption for their children) and birth parents (mothers and fathers who have placed their children for adoption), and considers the semantic and historical contexts for these issues. It addresses the process through which prospective birth parents reach the decision to place their children for adoption and the short- and long-term impact of these decisions on them. It next considers the legal issues bearing on consent to adoption, with a focus on birth mothers and birth fathers, and the implications of these issues for adoption practice. Consideration is then given to the impact of adoption on birth parents whose children are placed for adoption internationally and the impact of adoption on birth parents whose parental rights are involuntarily terminated. Finally, the trend toward greater openness in adoption is examined, with considerations related to the implications of open adoption for birth parents.

The Semantic Context

The issues related to the impact of adoption on birth parents are set within a context in which the very terms used to refer to these members of the triad and their decision-making are value-laden. The term "birth parent," for example, is commonly used in literature and in discussions of issues impacting the biological parents of children served through adoption. In reality, however, "birth parent" almost invariably refers only to birth mothers. Birth fathers receive comparatively little attention and, when referenced at all, generally are described as "alleged" or "putative" [Rosenberg 1992, p. 17]. The extent to which birth fathers have viable interests has been the subject of debate at both the legal and social service levels. This issue, addressed in more detail later in this volume, raises questions about the extent to which birth fathers are seriously viewed as "real" fathers or as "parents" at all.

The term "birth mother" is also used extensively in the literature, but its reference to women whose children are placed with adoptive families may be, in reality, both too broad and too narrow. On the one hand, the term "birth mother" often is used to encompass not only a woman who has placed her child for adoption, but a pregnant woman who is in the process of making the decision whether to raise her child herself or relinquish her child for adoption. As some commentators on this issue emphasize, pregnant women are "mothers" or, in the case of women considering adoption, "prospective birth mothers," just as those seeking to adopt are not yet "parents" but "prospective adoptive parents" [see Axness 1999a, p. 1; Axness & Shaw 1999]. Women become "birth mothers" only upon the completion of the adoption plan [Axness & Shaw 1999]. The tendency to refer to single pregnant women who are considering adoption as "birth mothers" may reflect a misunderstanding of their status or, in relation to ethical issues discussed later, may suggest certain expectations as to what these women's decisions should be.

The term "birth mother" also is used in a way that is quite narrow, generally referring only to women who themselves place their infants and very young children for adoption. Mothers of children in the foster care system whose parental rights are involuntarily terminated are rarely encompassed within the general meaning of the term "birth mother," and, consistent with this pattern, their interests and experiences rarely have been a focus of research or the social work or psychological literature. The absence of attention to the issues impacting this population of birth mothers reflects the relative invisibility of these birth parents in relation to adoption practice and policy, an issue also addressed later in this volume.

Although the terms "birth parent," "birth mother," and "birth father" are the customary terms for these members of the triad—irrespective of the limitations on their usage, some commentators have proposed other terminology. One author [Kadushin 1970], in a particularly harsh vein, refers to birth parents as "biological conceivers" and contends that they are not worthy of being called "parent" because they either on their own rejected that role or the title was taken from them because of their poor conduct. Spencer [1999, p. 13] proposes that more appropriate terms for birth mothers are "birthgiver," "woman who gave birth," and "genetic mother," and that more appropriate terms for a birth father are "man who shared in the conception" and "genetic father." Although she maintains that her proposed terms are "accurate" and "descriptive"—as opposed, for example, to the terms "biological mother" and "biological father" which she rejects—the difference is not readily discernible. Descriptions of birth parents in functional terms related to genetic contributions or conception-related activity may, in fact, convey an even more reductive view of birth parents.

At the same time, the language used to refer to decision-making by birth parents (birth mothers and birth fathers) also carries value-based judgments. Edwards [1999, p. 389] notes that the terms generally used to refer to the decision-making process such as "'surrender,' 'relinquish,' and 'release' are...powerful—and political." Although the term "surrender" is used less frequently in contemporary adoption practice, its widespread use through the early 1970s may quite accurately reflect how birth mothers experienced and may continue to experience the process leading to their children's adoptions. Edwards [1999, p. 389] notes that "surrender" denotes the women's sense of "a giving up of a battle they waged unsuccessfully." "Release," she [1999, p. 389] notes, is the newly preferred term on the part of many adoption facilitators and adoption parents. Edwards [1999, p. 389] views the term "release for adoption"—which she analogizes to "release from prison" or "release into flight"—with some skepticism, asking, "Release to or from what?" "Release" seems to suggest a "setting free" from undesirable circumstances—the care of the birth parents—to more favorable ones —the care of adoptive parents. Spencer argues to the contrary, suggesting that "release" accurately denotes "the reality that the adoption plan offered problem resolution for all parties involved" [1999, p. 16]. The difference in perspectives expressed by Edwards, a birth mother, and Spencer, an adoption professional, may rest on the nature of their experiences with adoption planning.

In this volume, the terms "relinquish" and "place for adoption" primarily will be used to refer to the process in which birth parents are engaged. The term "relinquish" may most aptly reflect the experience of birth parents for whom the adoption process was, to a greater or lesser degree, thrust upon them as a result of personal, social, or other factors. The term "place for adoption" may reflect the experiences of those birth parents for whom the adoption process was more of an independent and informed choice. It is recognized, however, that the term "place for adoption" may sanitize the emotional environment surrounding the decision-making process even in the best circumstances and may not reflect with complete accuracy the experience of birth parents. The terms "relinquish" and "place for adoption," nonetheless, are utilized in an attempt to avoid the negative implications of other terms that, in essence, suggest that birth parents "gave up" or "gave away" their children.

The Historical Context

Historically, the birth parent of primary concern has been the unmarried pregnant woman whose status, from a social perspective, has varied significantly over the course of the last century.

Solinger [1992] notes that in the early part of the century—until the late 1930s—social service agencies were primarily child-centered, and their work centered on ensuring, to the maximum extent possible, that children born illegitimately were raised by their birth mothers. At the same time, laws in a number of states endeavored to create supports that would minimize the need to separate children born out of wedlock and their mothers [U.S. Children's Bureau 1938]. As embodied in both the law and social norms, all birth mothers, irrespective of race, were expected to raise their illegitimate children [Solinger 1992]. As a consequence, adoption was an uncommon event in the United States during this period [Perry 1998].

There were significant social changes in the post-Depression and post-World War II era, particularly in attitudes about women. Solinger [1992, p. 21] attributes the nature of the social climate in this period to a "concern for masculinity," specifically with regard to "the postwar capacities of adult males to sustain their traditional role of dominance in the family and in the culture at large." These concerns largely translated into criticisms of women whom society began to hold responsible for virtually all forms of "social diseases," including unwed motherhood [Solinger 1992, p. 21]. May [1988] describes a cultural uneasiness at the time about the independence that women had experienced during the war and a particular worry that single women, having experienced such independence, would engage in unbridled sex. Unwed motherhood represented the ultimate form of the excessive and irresponsible independence that society feared women would exhibit. Unwed mothers, consequently, were both attacked and marginalized—for violating multiple social rules regarding femininity, marriage and pregnancy and, perhaps most disturbingly, for reducing men through their conduct to "biological accessories" [May 1988, pp. 96-97]. As observed by a director of a home for single mothers in the 1940s and 1950s, society in that era viewed "illegitimacy as an inroad on the family's stability and permanency, and repel[led] it by ostracizing the unwed mother" [Edlin 1954, pp. 128-129].

The postwar era also saw a splitting in societal attitudes regarding Caucasian and African American single mothers. The Aid to Families with Children (AFC) program, established by the Social Security Act in 1935 and then extended to some children of unwed mothers in 1939, began to grow significantly in the 1940s. States began to seek ways to constrain the costs of the AFC program through limiting the financial assistance available to recipients. Many states targeted African American women whom they viewed as the principal abusers of AFC benefits at the taxpayer's expense [Solinger 1992]. Efforts to punish African American women, particularly those who had more than one illegitimate child, escalated through the 1950s and 1960s. By the early 1960s, a significant number of states had enacted or attempted to enact laws that prescribed incarceration or sterilization of women who had given birth to more than one child out of wedlock [Bell 1965; Littlewood 1977]. The harsh nature of these policies caused many African American leaders to denounce them as reflective of both racism and retribution against the growing civil rights movement [National Urban League 1960]. Solinger [1992] notes that these developments placed single African American pregnant women in a far more vulnerable position than their Caucasian counterparts. She [1992, p. 23] writes:

> The triple vulnerability of black women, defined by their race, their gender, and their childbearing age, created a climate of viciousness and danger for them even more than for white unwed mothers who were pariahs in their own communities.

As welfare and family support policy in the 1940s began to target African American single mothers as a major cause of society's problems, social service responses to unwed pregnancy began to diverge on the basis of the mother's race. The child-centered focus of the 1930s had gradually evaporated by the 1940s, and a "woman-centered" approach had emerged with its focus on managing the physical and social realities of an unwed pregnancy [Solinger 1992]. Equally important, illegitimacy began to be differentially defined in race-specific terms. Single Caucasian women who became pregnant were viewed as having psychological problems, not sexual desires [Ripple 1953]. By contrast, illegitimacy in the African American community was seen as the result of the uncontrolled sexual activity of single African American women, a view that admitted no psychological dimension whatsoever [Solinger 1992].

These differing race-based views of illegitimacy had significant implications for pregnancy counseling services and the extent to which adoption was viewed as an appropriate response to an unwed pregnancy. Based on the prevailing psychological view of illegitimacy for unmarried Caucasian women, adoption was deemed appropriate. These women, by virtue of their psychological problems, were "by definition, unfit mothers, in fact not mothers at all" [Solinger 1992, p. 24]. The fact that they had become pregnant outside of marriage was evidence of a psychological condition that preempted them from motherhood. They were expected, consequently, to place their babies for adoption for the sake of both their own and their babies' futures [Solinger 1992]. This view was further strengthened by the notion that Caucasian women could be rescued through adoption from their state of "shame" by atoning for the "wrong" through "casework treatment in a maternity home, relinquishment of the baby for adoption, and rededication...to the marriage market" [Solinger 1992, p. 25]. Adoption, consequently, provided the means for Caucasian women to avoid societal censure as "promiscuous" and morally "tainted" if the truth became known and protected their future prospects for marriage or career [Cole & Donley 1990, p. 284].

Caucasian women who resisted and chose to parent their children rather than place them for adoption were considered highly immature or, in the view of some, mentally ill [Meyer et al. 1959]. The literature of the era consistently characterized Caucasian mothers who kept their children—as opposed to women who made adoption plans—as less stable and more emotionally needy or, even more seriously, portrayed them as social deviants or "members of a subculture whose mores were at variance with those of society at large" [Grow 1979, p. 363]. Consistent with these views, women who opted to raise their children as single parents were subjected to the harshest of social sanctions. Solinger [1992, p. 33] writes:

> The white woman who kept was...violating consumerist principles. She was robbing society of the payment her deviance required...Segments of the public...found it morally satisfying to extract the only payment possible: the women who kept her child had to pay with her reputation and with community ostracism.

Despite the strong, if not unrelenting, social pressure and the high value placed on adoption during this era, it appears that adoption was not at any time the preferred option of unmarried pregnant Caucasian women [Kadushin 1980]. Although others cite higher rates [see Deykin et al. 1984; Resnick 1984], Chandra and associates [1999] in their comprehensive analysis of relinquishment rates, found that even in the 1960s and 1970s, when the placement rate of infants for adoption by unmarried mothers was relatively high, only 19% of unmarried Caucasian women made adoption plans. These data suggest that, as powerful as the pressures may have been on unmarried Caucasian women to place their children for adoption through the early 1970s, there were countervailing values that disfavored adoption as an option.

In contrast to societal expectations that unmarried Caucasian women would place their babies for adoption, African American women were expected to keep their babies and raise them themselves. Historically, African American single women rarely placed their children for adoption on a formal basis but, instead, turned to members of their extended families who informally assumed responsibility for their relative children [Perry 1998]. Because many children were the product of the rape of African American women by Caucasian men during slavery and after emancipation, African American communities generally did not stigmatize illegitimate children as did Caucasian communities—a pattern that continued beyond emancipation [Perry 1998]. Broader social attitudes, however, were far more critical. During the postwar era, in particular, unmarried pregnancy among African American women became subject to the harsh disapproval of Caucasian society. Out-of-wedlock births by single African American women were viewed as indicative of their sexual irresponsibility—as opposed to the psychological problems that caused illegitimate Caucasian births—and African American women were blamed for their condition, rather than shamed as were Caucasian women for their indiscretion [Solinger 1992].

Solinger [1992] writes that by the end of World War II, single pregnant African American women had become scapegoats for a host of societal problems, including the growing costs of welfare, the presence of unwanted children in U.S. society, and the endemic poverty among African Americans. In this environment, single African American women—in contrast to single, pregnant Caucasian women who could be redeemed through adoption—faced retribution [Solinger 1992]. They had to be punished for their "wrong"—to "pay dearly for the bad bargain they foisted on society, especially white taxpayers" through their efforts to "get something (benefits under the Aid to Dependent Children program) for nothing (another black baby)" [Solinger 1992, p. 30]. African American women who attempted to subvert this societal expectation and place their children for adoption encountered a harsh response. Many of these women were charged with desertion or were otherwise forced to support their children as punishment for their conduct [Solinger 1992]. Extremely few African American infants were placed for adoption during this period, exceeding no more than 1.5% of all nonmarital births [Chandra et al. 1999].

The distinction that adoption service providers made between Caucasian and African American infants was clearly influenced by race-based social attitudes and public policies. It also, however, was affected by the growing demand for Caucasian infants by infertile Caucasian couples. Solinger [1992] notes that although single pregnant women of both races were viewed through the 1970s as "breeders," the nature of the demand for infants created two distinct groups of unwed mothers. Single African American women were seen as "socially unproductive" breeders of children as their infants were not in demand by prospective adoptive parents [Solinger 1992, p. 24]. By contrast,

Caucasian women were "socially productive" breeders because their babies—viewed as having been conceived, unfortunately, without the benefit of marriage—nevertheless could provide infertile Caucasian couples with the opportunity to have a "proper family" [Solinger 1992, p. 24].

The public policies and social work practices of the 1940s and 1950s, despite their grounding on a view of "single pregnant women and unwed mothers as resources and as scapegoats," largely failed to change the reproductive behavior of young women [Solinger 1992, p. 39]. To the contrary, rates of unmarried child bearing continued to rise, and by the 1960s, abortion began to be given serious consideration in a number of state legislatures [Solinger 1992]. Solinger [1992, p. 39] writes that the differing, race-based definitions of illegitimacy in the postwar era, ironically, "helped define the way for women to make their own decisions." She [1992, p. 39] concludes:

> There is no question but that the state's authoritarian, postwar attitudes and policies toward single, pregnant girls and women stimulated thousands of women in the 1960s and 1970s to construct reproductive freedom as a feminist issue.

It is clear that in the 1970s, there were pronounced shifts in societal attitudes about sexual behavior, sexual relationships, and family. Premarital sex became more acceptable, marriage was seen as less necessary, and the traditional two-parent family no longer necessarily held preferred status [Grow 1979]. Women advocated for and achieved greater mobility and access to higher level jobs, which greatly enhanced their economic freedom. Families became more diverse as divorce rates increased, and children, to a far greater extent, were reared by single mothers. The negative connotations of single parenthood began to diminish, and the social stigma associated with "illegitimate" pregnancy no longer placed pressures on women to consider adoption [Cole & Donley 1990]. At the same time, women's rights, including the right to use contraceptives and obtain an abortion, made adoption less of an option of choice [Cole & Donley 1990].

With these political, social, and economic changes in women's status, social work views of unmarried mothers who raised their children and single women who placed their children for adoption also began to shift. Jacokes [1965] was among the early researchers to question the theory that women who placed their children for adoption were more psychologically stable than women who chose to parent. Festinger [1971], in her study of 137 pregnant, single teens, also disputed the theory that psychological factors were primary in decision-making by pregnant adolescents, and concluded instead that multiple forces affected their plans. She rejected the characterization of parenting teens as "deviant" and those who placed their children for adoption as "nondeviant." Similarly, Grow [1979], in her research, found little support for the explanation that social deviancy and psychological debilitation caused unmarried Caucasian women to decide to parent their children. She found that different social milieus characterized the two groups of women: women who decided to parent their children were from social environments that questioned the need for marriage, and women who decided to place their children for adoption were from more traditional social environments. In contrast to the assumptions found in the literature of the previous two decades, she concluded that each woman was the "product of her environment and cannot be regarded as either psychologically or socially deviant" [1979, p. 370]. A multifaceted understanding of unmarried pregnant women's decision-making became more common, and by the 1980s, explanations of psychological debilitation and social deviancy for the decision to parent or place their children for adoption had all but disappeared from the literature [Leynes 1980; Resnick 1984; Weinman et al. 1989].

Since the early 1970s, there has been a sharp decline in the likelihood that an unmarried woman will decide to place her child for adoption. Prior to 1973, about one-fifth of unmarried Caucasian women relinquished their infants; between 1973 and 1981, only 7.5% of these women placed their children for adoption; between 1982 and 1988, the percentage had declined to 3.2%; and between 1989 and 1995, the percentage had dropped to only 1.7% [Chandra et al. 1999]. Among African American unmarried women, the rate at which children have been placed for adoption has always been extremely low as a result of historical, social, and political factors. The percentage of unmarried African American women relinquishing their children for adoption never exceeded 1.5% and reached nearly zero by 1995 [Chandra et al. 1999]. By the 1980s, the differential between African American and Caucasian women began to narrow significantly, a trend that continued through the mid-1990s. By the end of the century, the relinquishment rates for the two groups of women were essentially the same [Chandra et al. 1999].

At the same time, from a social and cultural perspective, birth parents have become considerably more visible, both socially and politically. In the mid-20th century, birth parents had no public presence or voice. During that era, society placed birth mothers in a role in which they had few choices or in which their choices were determined by others [Baran et al. 1977]. As a result of considerable pressures from their families and professionals, "birth mothers felt unable to react in any way other than to surrender their babies. Thus, to meet the needs of others, they relinquished not only their babies, but their ability to decide on their own" [Weintraub & Konstam 1995, p. 317]. As a result of a sense of personal powerlessness and potent social stigmas associated with unwed pregnancy, birth parents were virtually invisible.

Beginning in the 1970s, however, birth mothers and birth fathers began to step forward and publicly bring attention to issues that affected them in relation to the adoption planning itself and its impact on them. As Anne Brodzinsky [1990, pp. 298-299] writes, birth parents began "to emerge from long years of silence to express sorrow, anger, and regret which they associate[d] with their decision." In the United States, birth parents formed Concerned United Birthparents [CUB] in 1976 to provide support to birth mothers and birth fathers who had relinquished their children [Concerned United Birthparents 2000]. Their mission subsequently expanded to include adoption reform in law and policy, prevention of unnecessary family separations, and education of the public about adoption issues and realities [Concerned United Birthparents 2000]. Similarly, the Australian Relinquishing Mothers Society [ARMS] was established by birth mothers seeking to bring their personal and political struggles to the larger community [Inglis 1984]. In England, the Natural Parents' Support Group was formed to take an active role in influencing social policy related to birth parents' interests and rights [Mason & Selman 1997].

As adoption has become an option chosen by fewer prospective birth parents, and birth parents have become more vocal in expressing their interests and their objections to the way in which adoption professionals have served them in the past, there has been a mobilization of forces to counter the trend away from adoption planning by prospective birth parents. As reflected in the most recent edition of the *Adoption Factbook III* [1999]— published by the National Council for Adoption, a Washington, D.C. lobbying organization—socially and politically conservative segments of the adoption community have focused their efforts on increasing the number of prospective birth parents who place their children for adoption. These efforts include the promotion of counseling to bring a pregnant woman to the point at which she "can consider adoption because it is best for the child, regardless of how difficult it may be for her" [Styles 1999, p. 309]; revival of maternity homes for unmarried pregnant women to convince them of the benefits of adoption [Pierce 1999b]; and overcoming, as a "barrier" to adoption, the "fact...that the stigma of nonmarital childbearing and dependency on public assistance continues to be reduced" [Pierce 1999b, p. 563]. These efforts suggest an agenda that would reconstruct the sociocultural and adoption service environment of the 1950s and 1960s and, presumably, reverse the declining rates at which single women opt to relinquish their infants for adoption.

The literature does not well address the history of adoption from the perspective of birth parents whose rights are involuntarily terminated and birth parents whose children are adopted internationally. These birth parents, nonetheless, represent important groups of birth parents whose numbers have grown over the past several decades. Beginning in the 1970s, as the number of infants placed for adoption began to decline, the population of children in foster care began to rise [Sokoloff 1993]. Adoption became the plan for some of these children, but the characteristics and experiences of their birth parents have not been well documented. The first wave of international adoption took place in the 1950s following the Korean War, with subsequent waves of international adoption involving children from Latin America, Russia and the Eastern Republics, and China [Altstein & Simon 1991]. As with the birth parents of children in foster care subsequently placed for adoption, little is known about the birth parents of these children. These issues are discussed in greater depth in subsequent sections of this analysis of the impact of adoption on birth parents.

Infant Adoption: The Impact on Prospective Birth Parents, Birth Mothers, and Birth Fathers

Both the research and the psychological and social work literature provide some understanding of the impact of adoption on prospective birth parents and on birth mothers and birth fathers who place their children for adoption. The decision whether to parent or place for adoption has been explored to some extent in the research—although primarily in relation to unmarried teen women's decision-making. The psychological impact of the adoption decision likewise has been the subject of consideration, although, once again, primarily in relation to birth mothers. There appears to be some level of consensus in the clinical literature and research regarding the immediate effects of the relinquishment decision, but there is much greater variability in the research regarding the longer-term impact on birth parents. The limited research on the impact of adoption on birth fathers suggests that some of the prevailing assumptions about birth fathers require greater attention, although negative assessments of their role in the adoption planning process persist in the clinical literature.

Prospective Birth Parents: The Decision to Parent or to Place for Adoption

In line with the primary focus on the role of mothers—as opposed to fathers—in parenting in general [Rotundo 1985], research has principally focused on the decision of prospective birth mothers to parent their children or relinquish their children for adoption. In the U.S., researchers have been principally interested in the demographic characteristics of unmarried pregnant teen women, as opposed to older women, and the focus has been on the social and psychological factors that influence these young women's decisions. Although it is clear that a small and declining percentage of single pregnant adolescents decides in favor of adoption [Chandra et al. 1999], those adolescents who make such a decision have been found to fit generally within a certain demographic and socioeconomic profile. Research suggests that unmarried adolescent women who relinquish are more likely to:

- be non-Latino white [Bachrach et al. 1990];

- be an older teenager [Bachrach et al. 1992];

- have an intact family [Namerow et al. 1993];

- have a family member who is adopted [Resnick et al. 1990];

- have more years of education [Bachrach et al. 1992];

- have college-educated parents [Cushman et al. 1993]; and

- enjoy greater economic resources [Leynes 1980].

These characteristics tend to highlight the higher socioeconomic and educational status of single adolescent women who make adoption plans.

Consistent with this general profile of teen women who decide in favor of adoption, Bachrach, Stolley, and London [1992] found in their comprehensive analysis of predictors of relinquishment that a decision to place for adoption was more likely when a teen woman was older and the woman's mother had some college education. The researchers also identified what they called the "opportunity costs" of parenthood as a key factor in the adoption decision. When these costs were high at the time of pregnancy, particularly in relation to enrollment in and success at school, the woman was more likely to choose adoption. Bachrach [1986, p. 252] noted in an earlier article on the opportunity costs for women who weigh the alternatives of parenting and adoption for their infants that "women who make adoption plans may do so because they foresee economic opportunities with which child-bearing would interfere." The extent to which such economic considerations play a causal role in decision-making, however, is not clear. Bachrach [1986] notes that women who make the decision to place their children for adoption simply may have greater economic opportunities because they do not have family responsibilities.

Research has identified three other major influences on decision-making by unmarried pregnant teen women. First, several studies have found that the mother of the pregnant teenager most influences the decision that the young woman makes [Dworkin et al. 1993; Resnick 1984; Leynes 1980]. Through the 1980s, the mothers of pregnant teens were most likely to promote a decision in favor of adoption [Resnick 1984; Leynes 1980]. Second, studies have suggested that the father of the baby most influences the consistency of the plan to place or parent the child [Dworkin et al. 1993; Blum et al. 1987; Geber & Resnick 1988]. When the father is involved, his values have been found to have significant social, psychological, and economic consequences for the pregnant adolescent woman [Bachrach 1986]. Third, research has associated the residential environment of a maternity home with an increased likelihood that a teen woman will place her child for adoption. One study, for example, found that pregnant teen women who lived for any time during their pregnancies in a maternity facility were twice as likely to place their children for adoption than those who did not spend time in a residence [Namerow et al. 1993]. These factors suggest the powerful roles that both significant others and the service delivery system historically have played in an adolescent woman's decision-making regarding parenting or adoption.

Since the 1980s, single pregnant adolescents increasingly have made the decision to parent rather than place their babies for adoption. Between 10% and 20% of single pregnant adolescents placed their infants for adoption in the mid-1970s [Baldwin 1976]. Beginning in the 1980s, the rate declined so that by 1990, fewer than 4% of single pregnant adolescents relinquished their children [Bachrach 1986; Bachrach et al. 1990].

Explanations vary for the decline in decision-making in favor of adoption among this group of birth mothers. Some writers have focused on adolescents' social environment. Donnelly and Voydanoff [1996, p. 427], for example, attribute the declining rate of adoptive placements by young women to personal, familial, and peer factors:

> It is painful for most mothers—not only adolescents—to place the child they have borne. Often the adolescents' families pressure the young mothers to maintain custody of the child...Placing for adoption is such an uncommon decision among their peers that some adolescents have undoubtedly never even considered adoption an option for themselves.

Rosenberg [1992, p. 24] similarly suggests that young women may be "plagued with the incongruousness of thinking of themselves as loving parents and simultaneously giving a child away. There may be pressure from peers and others who see relinquishment as a selfish act." With regard to African American teen women, Kalmuss [1992] attributes the low rate of adoptive placements to multiple factors: relatively low opportunity costs associated with early childrearing, particularly when the woman perceives few educational or career options and parenting is viewed as the entry into the adult world; the relative absence of stigma in the African American community regarding unmarried parenting; and the involvement of extended family in the life of the mother and the child which may serve as a buffer to some of the risks associated with teen parenting. Mech [1986], by contrast, attributes the low level of interest in adoption among single pregnant adolescents to the attitudes of crisis pregnancy counselors. He found in his study that many counselors assume that an adolescent wishes to parent and find it difficult to present adoption as an option.

Research, to some extent, has considered the broader population of women with unplanned pregnancies who choose to parent or to make an adoption plan. In their study, Chippindale-Bakker and Foster [1996], for example, interviewed both adolescent and older unmarried women (ages 14 through 36) who received counseling services during their pregnancies and assistance in planning for their children. In examining the factors associated with the woman's decision to parent (the decision of 55.5% of the women) or to place her child for adoption (the decision of 44.4%), the researchers found three key influences. First, they found—consistent with the research conducted with unmarried teen women only—that the higher the level of education, the more likely the mother was to choose adoption. Second, they found that the involvement of the birth mothers' parents in the decision-making was a key influence, but not in the direction suggested by previous research. In their study, when the birth mothers' parents had influence in the decision-making process, it was more likely that the woman would choose parenting rather than, as indicated by earlier research, adoption. The researchers raised the possibility that with changes in broader social attitudes about single parenting, families may have become more supportive of keeping grandchildren within the family.

Finally, they found that contact with prospective adoptive parents—a variable not addressed in earlier research—was a key influence. When birth mothers chose and met the prospective adoptive parents, they were more likely to proceed with the adoption plan. In their interviews with birth mothers, the researchers found that meeting the prospective adoptive parents provided the mothers with the reassurance that adoption provided a better option for their children than what they themselves could provide and that the particular adoptive parents were the right choice for their children. This finding raises important issues regarding the impact of greater openness on birth parents, an issue that is discussed later in greater depth.

The research has touched on several other factors associated with decisions of the broader group of prospective birth mothers. Some researchers have suggested differences among women related to romanticism versus goal-orientation [Medora et al. 1993], and others have hypothesized the importance of anticipated psychological discomfort [Custer 1993]. The analyses of other researchers reflect their professional orientations, and as a consequence, raise questions about the substance of the findings. Bonnet [1993], a psychoanalyst, for example, theorized—on the basis of her study of 22 women—that a woman's choice of adoption was motivated in the majority of cases by "specific psychological mechanisms." Utilizing a psychoanalytic framework, Bonnet [1993, p. 509] emphasized factors at a deeper unconscious level, concluding that the women essentially feared harming their children and that adoption was "an act of love, for it protects the child." She further explained [1993, p. 509]:

> Violent fantasies toward the child are so terrifying that the women fear that ultimately they will not be able to contain them, and therefore will not love the child. They make the decision to part with the child in order to protect it from the risk of violence or neglect. It is all the more important for them to protect their child as they themselves have suffered as children at the hands of their parents. They cannot give love that they have never received...In giving up the child they are performing a unique maternal act, for they are identifying with the needs of the infant, protecting its life for the risk of violence or neglect, and giving it the chance to be loved by others.

The range of research findings—and the frameworks supporting them—suggest that multiple factors are likely to bear on a woman's decision to parent or to place her child for adoption. It is not clear—given the various theories advanced—to what extent the research sheds light on the decision-making process. It is clear, however, that fewer women are opting in favor of adoption. What is the impact of the decision to relinquish? Does an understanding of the short- and long-term impact of such decisions influence how birth parents view adoption as an option?

The Psychological Impact of the Adoption Decision on Birth Mothers

Although the social and cultural environment that influenced women's choices regarding adoption in the past has changed significantly over the past three decades, the complexities inherent in the role of "birth mother"—and the psychological impact of this role on women—do not appear to have diminished over time. Axness [1994, p. 7] observes that social stigma and stereotypes of birth mothers continue to play a powerful role. She [1994, p. 7] writes:

> I believe that in the adoption industry as it exists today, adoptive parents are tacitly encouraged to paternalisti- cally view the birth mother as less endowed economi- cally, educationally, culturally, sometimes even morally, and thus less equipped—and therefore less deserving— to parent.

Kirk [1985, p. 117] similarly notes that adoption—even in the current environment that may accord birth parents a fuller role in the decision-making process and beyond—has created ambiguity and provided, at best, "enigmatic answers" as birth mothers have continued to be put "in a dilemma of contradictory rules of conduct." The contradiction plays out, on the one hand, through the social prescription that a mother should always care for her child irrespective of the circumstances that she confronts [Kirk 1985]. On the other hand, there is the prevailing "professional rule" of practitioners and policymakers that a birth mother should, for the sake of her child and for her own well-being, place her child for adoption [Kirk 1985, p. 117]. These conflicting role expecta- tions create difficult dilemmas with long-term implications:

> [I]f she decides to surrender the child, what will this act mean to her in the years to come? Is she still a "mother"? Can she totally forget—can she put the surrender aside, and with it the birth, and the pregnancy? And if she cannot forget the fact of the surrender, how can she make sense of the fact that out there, somewhere is the child whom she has given life, but about whose life she knows nothing; and more, about whose life is not supposed to know anything? [Kirk 1985, p. 117].

Consistent with Kirk's observations, loss is an overarching theme in the psychological literature regarding the experiences of women who choose adoption for their children. This body of work suggests that loss is associated initially with the crisis pregnancy itself, both in terms of the physical demands of the pregnancy and the woman's awareness of the diminished respect of her family members, friends, and the community [Romanchik 1997b; Silverman 1981]. The sense of loss deepens as the woman finds herself having to make a decision about her child, a process that is likely to evoke "feelings of denial, fear, anger, awe and outright panic" [Romanchik 1997b, p. 2]. Rosenberg [1992, p. 25] writes that loss becomes particularly intense when adoption will likely be the outcome:

> For relinquishing parents, the entire pregnancy is fraught with issues of attachment and loss. At one extreme, some mothers decide to enjoy the attachment until the baby is gone; they live for today, nurturing the pregnancy and the baby in whatever ways they can while they have it. At the other extreme are those who try to deny any emotional attachment in an attempt to protect themselves from future loss. In between are those who experience attaching and having to let go at the same time. Each warm moment of response to the moving fetus is followed by another moment of anticipatory grief.

The decision to relinquish is likely to carry with it guilt and shame, each of which is associated with loss. Romanchik [1997b] writes that these two distinct emotions permeate the birth mother's current and future reality. She describes guilt as the "feeling that you did not do enough to keep your child with you"—a sense of complete responsibility for the loss of one's child [1997b, p. 2]. Shame, by contrast, is "not feeling worthy to be involved, not feeling worthy to parent again, not feeling worthy enough to demand respect as a birthparent" [Romanchik 1997b, p. 2]. Carol Schaefer's description of the emotions she felt upon seeing her son for the first time conveys her feelings of guilt and shame at that moment:

> The first time I looked into my son's eyes, I felt like a criminal. As I unwrapped his hospital blanket and took in

the fragrance of a newborn, I feared that the nurses or nuns would appear to accuse me of contaminating my own son. The three months I had spent at the home for unwed mothers had left me feeling I would be the worst person for my own child to know [1991, p. 292].

Rosenberg [1992, p. 31] similarly points to the guilt associated with the decision to relinquish, particularly given "the process of attachment that has existed throughout the pregnancy." She writes that birth parents' sense of guilt flows from having to "confront their own responsibility, for they created the circumstances of their own loss" [Rosenberg 1992, p. 33]. At the same time, feelings of guilt are likely to be intensified by the implicit judgments of others that birth parents made their problems and should not complain [Rosenberg 1992]. Gritter [1997] similarly highlights the underlying sense of shame that birth parents feel and the social environment that intensifies this feeling. He suggests that the shame that pervades birth parents' experiences is linked to five related factors: a sense of defectiveness; powerlessness in the process; self-perceptions of "dirtiness"; a sense of rejection; and depersonalization [1997, pp. 220-221]. He observes that "shame has been a fundamental motivator prompting birthparents to consider adoption" and accounts for the fact that many birth parents are, in essence, in "hiding" [1997, pp. 223-224].

Although there may be some agreement regarding the range of feelings that birth mothers experience at the time they relinquish their children, there is less agreement on the longer-term impact on women who make adoption plans. Two conflicting themes have emerged from the literature and research that have focused on outcomes for unmarried women who choose to parent their children and those who choose adoption. The first theme is that adoption is a traumatic experience for the mother with negative consequences for her future well-being and personal and social functioning. The second theme is that adoption, by providing a positive alternative for an unplanned pregnancy, benefits the unmarried mother on a long-term basis, as well as significantly benefiting her child.

The first theme, suggesting long-term negative effects for birth mothers, is most clearly developed in the empirical research from Australia. This research, which is so homogenous that it is often characterized as the "Australian" point of view [Curtis 1990], consistently has found that women who place their children for adoption are at significant risk of long-term physical, emotional, and interpersonal difficulties [Condon 1986; McHutchinson 1986; Van Keppel & Winkler 1983]. These studies suggest that many women who place their children for adoption suffer severe and debilitating grief that continues over time [Van Keppel & Winkler 1983]; experience ongoing problems in their relationships with men and difficulties in parenting subsequent children [Condon 1986]; adjust poorly or not at all to placing their children for adoption [Bouchier et al. 1991]; and often experience symptoms similar to posttraumatic stress disorder [Wells 1993]. Winkler and Van Keppel [1984], in their study of 213 birth mothers that included a control group of community women found that the effects of relinquishment were both negative and long lasting. One-half of the birth mothers stated that their sense of loss increased over time and extended, in the case of many women, over a 30-year time period. The researchers found that birth mothers suffered from significantly greater psychological impairment than the women in the control group, and that three factors were associated with the birth mothers' psychological distress: the lack of opportunities to talk with others about their feelings related to the adoption of their children; the absence of social supports; and a pervasive sense of loss regarding their children.

By contrast, research in the United States has tended to highlight the benefits of adoption, emphasizing the risks associated with unmarried parenting and the benefits of adoption for the mother and child [Curtis 1990]. Particularly with regard to unmarried teen mothers, many U.S. researchers have pressed adoption as the resolution for unplanned pregnancies and urged pregnancy counselors to promote adoption as an option, if not the preferred alternative under such circumstances [Mech 1986; Musick et al. 1984]. This body of research is not as uniform as the Australian research, however, and, as a result, it raises a number of questions regarding the longer-term outcomes for birth mothers.

Much of the U.S. research has suggested educational and economic benefits for single women when they choose adoption instead of parenting and important benefits for their children when they are placed with adoptive families. These studies, which primarily focus on teen women, tend to suggest that women who decide to parent their children are at heightened risk of lower educational achievement and lower rates of high school completion [Mott & Marsiglio 1985]; greater dependency on welfare benefits and poorer employment opportunities [Duncan & Hoffman 1990]; and higher divorce rates [Furstenberg et al. 1987]. Studies also have indicated negative outcomes for children raised by their adolescent mothers: poorer health, higher levels of poverty, lower educational achievement, greater frequency of behavioral problems, and a higher risk of early sexual activity and pregnancy [Hofferth 1987; Strobino 1987]. Summing up this body of research, Kalmuss [1992, p. 486] notes that the "research indicates that relinquishment offers potential benefits for the pregnant teenager and her baby," with the benefits for the mother being higher socioeconomic status and higher levels of marital stability, and the benefits for the child being higher socioeconomic status in their adoptive homes than would be the case if they were reared in a single-parent home.

In her analysis of the research, Kalmuss [1992, p. 486] recognizes that the socioeconomic benefits of relinquishment would be counterbalanced by research showing that birth mothers experience negative psychological consequences as a result of the decision to place their children for adoption. Like other writers in this area, however, she maintains that "such data do not exist" [1992, p. 486]. She argues that methodological problems undermine findings that suggest that birth mothers experience long-term feelings of grief and loss or diminished psychological functioning [see Deykin et al. 1984; Sorosky et al. 1984], and she highlights the research that shows that women who place their infants for adoption fare no worse psychologically than those women who parent their children [McLaughlin et al. 1988a, 1988b].

Some U.S. research, however, offers a point of departure to this positive interpretation of the longer-term impact of relinquishment on birth mothers. Some research finds mixed outcomes for unmarried teen women who choose parenting or adoption. Namerow and colleagues [1993], for example, compared unmarried teen women who placed their children for adoption and women who parented their children four years after the decision. Those women who chose to place their children had a higher overall satisfaction with life; scored higher on such factors as employment, finances, and the quality of their relationships with their partners; and reported a more positive future outlook [Namerow et al. 1993]. They also found, however, that teen women who placed their children for adoption reported a greater degree of regret about their decision [Namerow et al. 1993]. Similarly, McLaughlin [1988b], in a study of 269 adolescent mothers (146 who relinquished and 123 who chose to parent), found that women who placed their children for adoption had higher levels of education, were more likely to be employed, and had higher household incomes. Both groups reported satisfaction with their respective decisions, although the women who decided in favor of adoption were less satisfied than the women who chose to parent. Neither the studies of Namerow and colleagues [1993] nor McLaughlin [1988b] followed the women longitudinally to assess longer-term outcomes.

Other research—more in line with the Australian studies—has focused on longer-term outcomes and found decidedly more negative outcomes for women who place their children for adoption. Edwards [1995], for example, found a range of poor psychological outcomes in her study of 56 birth mothers who relinquished 16 to 51 years ago. She found that the women shared a number of early traumatic experiences: problematic relationships with their mothers or stepmothers whom they perceived as critical, hostile, cold, unloving, or abusive [67.8%]; childhood physical, sexual, or emotional abuse [71%]; the death of a parent prior to the pregnancy [23%]; and abandonment by one or both parents (other than through death) at some point in childhood [16%]. She identified, consistent with other research, five principal factors leading to the women's decisions to place their children for adoption: rejection by the baby's father; rejection by their own parents or the fathers' parents; demands by their own parents and the birth fathers to place their children for adoption; pressure from social workers and other authority figures to place their children for adoption; and lack of emotional and material support for parenting.

The participants' descriptions of their experiences after placing their children for adoption suggested an ongoing sense of loss. The women frequently described the experience of placing their children for adoption as the most traumatic event of their lives; related multiple symptoms of posttraumatic stress; and expressed a desire for search and reunion in order to fully heal. Almost three-quarters [73%] of the women who had found or been found by their children felt disappointed by the way their children had been raised and a sense that their children did not have the promised "ideal" adoptive families.

In addition to Edwards' study, other research supports clinical observations of "the pain, guilt and frustration which birth mothers never cease to suffer and the lack of sympathy or understanding they learn to expect" [Harris and Whyte 1999, p. 47]. Weintraub and Konstam [1995], for example, interviewed a small group of birth mothers who had placed their infants for adoption during the 1960s and 1970s and found that they consistently reported pain associated with secrecy and isolation, a sense of stigmatization and personal disgrace, depression, perceptions of failures in relationships, difficulty "moving on" with their lives, and dissatisfaction with the services they received from helping professionals. Based on her research, Anne Brodzinsky [1990, p. 309], characterizing the experiences of birth mothers as "nearly universal," observed:

> Typically, these women have been advised by caseworkers, family members, and lawyers that their baby would be better off with people who can take "proper" care of a child and that the best thing for them to do would be to place their child for adoption and go on with their lives with the comforting knowledge that they have made the

best possible plan for their baby. These assumptions and imposed solutions represent variations on a common theme which support abnegation of personal ideals and suppression of feelings in these young mothers.

She [1990, p. 309] found that a significant number of mothers who relinquished their infants "experience[d] pathological grief reactions which interfere with their overall functioning for a good portion, and possibly the remainder of their lives."

The Impact of Adoption on Birth Fathers

Neither the research nor the literature extensively address the role of the birth father in adoption nor the effects on a birth father of the decision to place his child for adoption [Clapton 1997]. Mason [1995b, p. 29] writes that "the birth father continues to be the least represented, least considered and least heard in adoption literature, conferences and advocacy efforts." Because the research is limited and has primarily focused on teenage fathers and not on single fathers as a group [see Card & Wise 1981; Deykin et al. 1988], the role of birth fathers in planning for their children and the impact on birth fathers of the adoption decision are not well understood. Nonetheless, the consensus is that birth fathers are uninvolved in and unconcerned about planning for their children [Lightman & Schlesinger 1982] and that they remain unaffected by decisions related to the adoptive placements of their children [Mason 1995a]. In the words of one adoption service provider, the "typical characteristic of a birth father is that he is unknown or that he is not involved in the adoption plan for the infant" [Daly & Sobol 1994, p. 89].

The current body of research suggests that multiple factors bear on birth fathers' involvement in decision-making about their children. Deykin and colleagues [1988], in a nonrepresentative sample of birth fathers identified through postadoption support and advocacy groups, found that a little over half did not participate in the decision-making regarding their children, and most (64%) had no contact with the child prior to the adoptive placement. In examining the factors related to the birth fathers' lack of active involvement in, if not exclusion from, the adoption process, they found that the absence of birth fathers from the process was associated with four major factors: pressures from their families, a poor relationship with the birth mother, financial issues, and the attitudes of adoption agencies.

Menard [1997] similarly emphasizes the relationship between the birth mother and birth father in influencing the father's involvement in the adoption process. She found that the role of the birth father was most clear when he had a positive relationship with the birth mother and together they decided that adoption was the best plan for their child. In the absence of such a relationship, the birth father's role was less clearly defined and was determined differently in each case, whether by the birth father himself, the birth mother, or the adoptive parents who, for example, in some cases wished to meet the birth father even if the birth mother objected [Menard 1997]. The marked variability in the role played by birth fathers may be associated with the ambiguity surrounding men's roles in family matters in general. Saunders [1996], for example, points to the lack of positive role models for men, not only in the context of adoption planning, but in their relationships with their children when there is divorce and remarriage and in relationships created through reproductive technologies, such as sperm donation, in-vitro fertilization, and surrogacy.

The adoption research and literature presents varying assessments of birth fathers and the impact of adoption planning on these men. Cicchini, in his study of birth fathers in Western Australia [1993], interviewed 30 men who volunteered in response to articles and public appeals. As in the study by Deykin and associates [1988], Cicchini explored the men's involvement in the decision-making process and found that the majority (66%) had no or only minimal say in the adoption. He also sought information on the long-term impact of the adoption on the birth fathers and found that they consistently viewed relinquishment as "a most distressing experience" [1993, p. 18]. He [1993, p. 18] concluded:

> The most significant finding is that the relinquishment experience does not end at the time of adoption, but has

enduring effects throughout life . . . These effects emerge most clearly decades later in a desire to be reunited with the child and seek assurance that the child is all right.

Romanchik [1997b] writes that the process by which birth parents experience the loss of the role of "parent" is significantly different for birth mothers and birth fathers. She states that birth fathers experience shame and grief as do birth mothers, but in a different manner because they are physically removed from the pregnancy and, as a result, only abstractly involved with the reality of the child. After the child's birth, they may hesitate to express their wishes regarding their child out of a fear of rejection, or they may see their role in decision-making as largely secondary, with the expectation that they merely will be "told what they are required to do" [Romanchik 1997b, p. 2]. Romanchik [1997b, p. 2] notes that although there are some birth fathers who are abusive to their children's birth mothers and should be approached with caution, the majority are "ostracized because of problems that occur within their personal relationship with the birth mother"—problems that are predictable given the stresses that accompany any pregnancy and, particularly, a crisis pregnancy.

Mason [1995a], in her book *Out of the Shadows: Birthfathers' Stories*, writes that views of birth fathers have been distorted by a number of myths. One prevailing belief is that birth fathers are not as connected to their children as are birth mothers. Her interviews with birth fathers revealed less of an absence of connection and more of a feeling of uncertainty regarding the role they should play in a crisis pregnancy—a theme similarly suggested by Saunders [1996]. She also found that many birth fathers believed that biology gave them fewer rights to the child than the mother. A second prevailing belief is that birth fathers are uniformly unaccountable, irresponsible, and absent during and after the pregnancy. She found in her interviews with birth fathers that they had ongoing thoughts and concerns about their children, a finding that undermined the belief that men move on with their lives, easily forgetting the child. She discovered that the lack of involvement on the part of birth fathers was associated to some extent with the practice of many adoption agencies of discouraging birth fathers from connecting with their children before consenting to the adoption. Mason [1995a] also found that birth fathers often depersonalized the experience of the pregnancy, birth, and planning for the child in order to emotionally and physically distance themselves from pain and uncertainty. Some developed amnesic states about the pregnancy and birth, reporting an inability to remember any details, and others distanced themselves by referring to the child as "it." She found, however, in the case of every birth father she interviewed that there was a sense of shame at not being able to assume the role of "Dad" [1995a, p. 15].

Apart from the limited research on the role of birth fathers in adoption planning and its longer-term impact on these men are social attitudes about birth fathers that shape adoption law and policy, an issue discussed later in greater detail. At one end of this spectrum is the National Association for Birth Fathers and Adoption Reform, an organization that takes a strong advocacy position on behalf of birth fathers. This group argues that birth fathers are both willing and able to assume responsibility for their children but are affirmatively prevented from asserting their interests in their children because birth mothers and adoption professionals work to exclude them from the decision-making process. The birth father members of this group contend that they are penalized because they often lack the resources to "fight" affluent adoptive parents who are able to "wear [the birth father] down" and eventually "beat" him through protracted court proceedings [O'Neill 1994, p. 12]. They advocate legal and policy changes to better protect the interests of birth fathers.

Others, however, contend that there are few indicators of birth fathers' willingness to become involved in the adoption planning process, and they dismiss the influence of outside forces on birth fathers' level of participation in planning for their children. Anne Brodzinsky [1990, p. 315], for example, writes that:

> Interested, committed birth fathers remain in the minority, with most individuals who father a child outside the protection of marriage continuing in the centuries-old tradition of abdication of responsibility. Perhaps increased legal protec-

tion and psychological sensitivity will provide the support necessary for birth fathers to come forward in grater numbers, but until such time as that occurs, it is clear that the major burden of this enormous responsibility remains with the mother of the child.

Her view appears to be shared by the general public. In a 1997 survey of Americans' attitudes about adoption, respondents were far more likely to characterize birth fathers, as compared to birth mothers, as irresponsible and uncaring [Evan B. Donaldson Adoption Institute 1997].

Birth fathers who attempt to become involved in planning for their children against the objections of birth mothers, adoption agencies, or adoptive parents are subject to particular criticism. As Gritter notes [1997, p. 273], "we are disgusted when fathers bail out on their responsibilities but, as far as adoption is concerned, we are even more indignant when they show interest." Their interventions when adoption plans have been made are generally attributed to a variety of motives unconnected with a genuine desire to parent. Schwartz [1986], for example, maintains that birth fathers typically intervene out of a pride in paternity, which prompts them to attempt to keep their children within the family; a commitment to care for their children that primarily is related to their own personal experiences of being abandoned by their own fathers; cultural values that make adoption unacceptable; and anger at the birth mothers. Prager [1999, p. 363] maintains that these men "love their seed first" and not their children.

The Impact of Adoption on Birth Parents: Legal Issues

The issues that impact birth parents are shaped not only by societal attitudes about birth mothers and birth fathers and by adoption practice, but also by adoption law. Constitutional principles as well as state statutes and case law play significant roles in defining the rights of birth parents and the extent to which their interests in their children exist and are recognized. The legal rights of parents were first acknowledged by the United States Supreme Court in 1923 when, in *Meyer v. Nebraska,* the Court held that parents had the right to "marry, establish a home, and bring up children" [1923, p. 399]. That right subsequently was held to include the rights of parents to educate their children [*Wisconsin v. Yoder* 1972] and make reproductive decisions [*Griswold v. Connecticut* 1965]. In the 1970s, the Supreme Court expanded these rights—which previously only had been applied to married couples—to unmarried parents and held that all birth parents held a liberty interest in the custody and care of their children [Craig 1998]. Birth mothers' constitutional rights are clearly defined and protected, reflecting the unique physical and social relationship between a mother and her child. The Supreme Court held in both *Planned Parenthood v. Casey* [1992] and *M.L.B. v. S.L.J.* [1996] that a woman's rights upon giving birth rise to the level of due process and are therefore entitled to full constitutional protection. Women, as a consequence, have recognized constitutional rights to make decisions regarding their pregnancies and regarding their children, including the right to make an adoption plan if they so choose [Craig 1998].

The rights of birth fathers are less clear. In 1983 [*Lehr v. Robinson* 1983, p.261], the Supreme Court held that the "mere existence of a biological link" is not sufficient to bestow full constitutional protections on a birth father. When a birth father is married to the birth mother or is the legal father of a child (as in the case of the husband of the biological mother), he receives the same due process and equal protection of his constitutional rights as the birth mother [Craig 1998]. When a birth father, however, is not married to the birth mother and has not established himself legally as the father of the child, he has only an "opportunity interest"— that is, a less-than-absolute right to the possibility of a parental relationship with his child [Craig 1998]. Although states are required to protect an unmarried father's interest in establishing such a parental relationship, they are free to define the specific conduct in which an unmarried father must engage in order to demonstrate that he has indeed assumed a parental role in his child's life [Craig 1998].

These legal principles have been well established by the Supreme Court [*Stanley v. Illinois* 1972; *Quillon v. Walcott* 1978; *Caban v. Mohammed* 1979; *Lehr v. Robinson* 1983]. The Court, however, has not addressed the extent to which a birth father has a right to consent to or veto an adoption when he has not developed the type of relationship that gives rise to constitutionally protected rights because he was denied the opportunity to do so. As a consequence, it is unclear to what extent birth fathers have rights in two types of cases—those in which the birth father has no knowledge of the pregnancy because the birth mother has not communicated that information to him, and cases in which the birth father is aware of the pregnancy but the birth mother informs him that she has miscarried or the child died in childbirth when, in reality, she has placed the child for adoption. These situations raise legal and ethical issues related to parental consent to adoption and have generated considerable debate. Some commentators suggest that the rights of birth fathers to object to an adoption when these situations arise should be significantly limited [Bartholet 1993b]. Others maintain that unknowing birth fathers should not lose the opportunity to parent, arguing that such an outcome would not be acceptable in any other set of circumstances [Hamilton 1987/1988].

These issues arise in their most highly contentious form when birth fathers assert their interests after an infant has been placed with an adoptive family. In most of the cases that have come to the attention of the media and public, a birth father, previously unknown to the adoption agency or attorney or the prospective adoptive parent, claims that his consent to the adoption was required but was not obtained and that he wishes to parent his child. Some cases have involved the additional circumstance that the birth mother, who previously consented to the adoption, wishes to revoke her consent or contest its validity. These cases raise questions regarding the extent to which birth parents should be informed of their rights in giving consent to adoption; should be given the opportunity to change their minds after making an adoption plan for their children; and, in the case of unmarried birth fathers, should be given the latitude to assert their rights when they were not allowed to participate in the decision-making process related to parenting or adoption. On the one hand, it is argued that birth parents' rights and opportunities in these matters should be significantly constricted because of the harm to children when such situations develop [see Gill 1991; Scarnecchia 1995]. In this vein, the argument is made that children are subjected to uncertainty and potential disruption in their lives and experience long-term harm as a result of contested situations between birth and adoptive parents. On the other hand, it is argued that birth parents' rights and opportunities must be respected and that neither the interests of children nor their families are served by a process that undermines the interests of birth parents in raising their children [see Appell & Boyer 1995].

The public largely has become aware of the potential for contested adoptions through high profile cases, such as *Baby Jessica* and *Baby Richard*. The media tends to focus on the issues in these cases from the perspective of the adoptive family and, to a great extent, that viewpoint has shaped the public debate. A review of newspaper articles on the subject reveals that media reporting typically sympathizes with adoptive families in their efforts to keep the child with them when a birth parent intervenes and harshly judges, if not vilifies, the birth parent [see Goodman 1993]. Birth parents generally are portrayed as deceitful, irresponsible, and unworthy of their children, characterizations that have shaped public attitudes and prospective adoptive parents' perceptions. In a survey in *Roots and Wings* [1996], for example, the editors sought via the Internet responses to the question, "Why did you choose one route to adoption over another?" Several families stated that they had chosen to adopt internationally rather than domestically because of the concern about a possible disruption of a domestic adoption. They [1996, pp. 28-29] described "the real fear of a birth mother coming back to get her baby after placement;" "worry" about the chance of losing a child because a birth parent would change his or her mind;" and unwillingness to "risk the possible difficulties we might encounter with birth parents who might reclaim their child."

Although the extent to which adoptions are contested is extremely limited [O'Neill 1994], when they do arise, they generally have involved practices that violate birth parents' rights at some level. The *Baby Jessica* case [*In re Baby Girl Clausen* 1993] provides such a case example, reflecting the key issues that can significantly impact the interests of both birth mothers and birth fathers in relation to adoption planning.

Cara Clausen, the birth mother of "Baby Jessica," was in her late 20s and unmarried when she discovered she was pregnant. She attempted to hide her pregnancy from family and friends and obtained no counseling about her options prior to giving birth. The Iowa-based lawyer who facilitated the adoption agreed to handle the adoption as a favor to a friend whose relatives, the DeBoers, wanted to adopt and who, though living in Michigan, had decided to adopt outside of the state. Although Iowa law provided that a valid consent to adoption could not be executed by the mother until at least 72 hours after a child's birth, the lawyer allowed Ms. Clausen to sign in his presence within 40 hours of giving birth. He did not explain to Ms. Clausen or to the man whom Ms. Clausen originally named as the father that the consent might be voidable because it was executed prior to the required 72 hours. Nor did he inform Ms. Clausen that she and the named birth father had a right to attend a judicial hearing in which their parental rights would be terminated based on their consents. The judicial proceeding went forward in Iowa a few days after Ms. Clausen signed the consent form, at which time the rights of Ms. Clausen and the man she named as father were terminated. The DeBoers were given permission to take the baby to Michigan.

Several days after signing the consent, Ms. Clausen communicated to the lawyer that she had made a mistake and wished to reclaim her child. She was aware that the lawyer had failed to comply with Iowa law regarding the taking of her consent and failed to inform her of her right to attend the termination of parental rights hearing. The case, however, was further complicated by issues related to consent by the birth father of her child. When Ms. Clausen filed a petition—within 10 days of signing the

consent—seeking to revoke her consent and set aside the termination of parental rights order, she also filed an affidavit stating that
she had lied about the identity of the child's birth father and that
Dan Schmidt was the true father of her child. At that point, Mr.
Schmidt filed an affidavit of paternity and sought to intervene in
the proceeding, opposing the adoption and asking that the proceeding be dismissed as his consent was lacking. Ultimately, after
years of litigation, the court held in Mr. Schmidt's favor. The court
found that Mr. Schmidt could not have known of the child's
existence until after the adoptive placement; once he learned that
he was the probable father, he did all that he could to legally
intervene and claim custody; and blood tests determined his
paternity.

The facts of this case and the court's decision raise a number
of questions related to birth parent decision-making, particularly
in the context of the legal principles governing consent and
revocation of consent. These issues are discussed in the following
section. The implications for adoption practice—in relation to the
services that are provided to prospective birth parents to ensure
informed decision-making—are also considered.

Consent and revocation of consent

Baby Jessica raises two sets of consent-related issues: the
validity of birth mothers' consent and the failure to accord birth
fathers the opportunity to plan for and either give or withhold
consent to the adoption. Both issues have played important
roles in contested adoption cases. Legally, the rule is that the
consent of birth parents must be obtained before an adoption
may validly take place unless parental rights have been waived
or involuntarily terminated [Hollinger 1999b]. Each state deter-
mines by statute the time at which a consent to adoption may be
given, the procedures to be followed, the time period during
which consent may be set aside by the birth parent, and the
grounds for revoking a consent to adoption. There is, however,
considerable variation among the states in each of these areas—
a situation that has raised a number of issues about both the

substance of the provisions in some states' laws and the fact that the variability may encourage parties to "shop" among states to avail themselves of more favorable provisions.

Birth Mothers' Consent. Most state statutes provide that a birth mother may give her consent to adoption only after the birth of her child, but the required waiting period ranges significantly—from allowing consent to be taken immediately after birth to a waiting period of a minimum of 15 days after birth [Hollinger 1999b]. As was the case in *Baby Jessica*, a fairly common provision among states is a waiting period of at least 72 hours [Hollinger 1999b]—a time period considered by some to be appropriate [see Gitlin 1987] and by others to be far too short [Lowe 1999]. Lowe [1999, p. 32], for example, questions the fairness of this time frame, asking, "Is 72 hours enough time to decide whether you can surrender your child forever?" In *Baby Jessica*, the lawyer did not wait even the required 72 hours after the baby's birth, but took the consent less than two days after Ms. Clausen had delivered her baby.

Questions about the procedures for taking a birth mother's consent likewise are raised by the case. States vary in the extent to which their statutes address the form of the consent, the information to be given to birth parents prior to consent, and the individuals who are authorized to take a consent [Hollinger 1999b]. Some state statutes do not require disclosure to birth parents of their rights related to consent [Hollinger 1999b]. Even in states where such disclosure is mandated, it is clear, as the *Baby Jessica* case illustrates, that compliance with such provisions cannot be assumed. Ms. Clausen, for example, was not informed about her right to attend the judicial hearing at which her parental rights would be terminated. Whether because he was unfamiliar with the adoption laws of the state or he represented the prospective adoptive parents (and not Ms. Clausen), the lawyer taking the consent never conveyed that information.

Concerns related to the taking of consents shortly after labor and delivery, the failure to advise birth parents of the full range of their rights, and the role of the adoptive parents' attorney in taking birth parents' consents are presented squarely in the *Baby Jessica* case. These issues are addressed in the Uniform Adoption Act (UAA), approved by the National Conference of Commissioners on Uniform State Laws in 1994, but as of 2000, not enacted in its entirety by any state. Specifically, the UAA provides that:

- a birth parent's consent is not valid until at least eight days after the child's birth and within that time, the birth parents have an unqualified right to reclaim the child;

- only a disinterested third party may take a consent to adoption and in no case may the lawyer representing the adoptive family take a consent; and

- the person taking a consent must explain to the birth parents the meaning of adoption and the consequences of the consent and attest to the apparent validity of the consent.

Although not directly raised in relation to Ms. Clausen's consent, the question of whether consent is given in a free and informed manner is an issue that has considerable relevance, particularly when a birth mother's consent is taken shortly after labor and delivery. Under the case law of virtually all states, a birth parent may challenge the validity of her consent if she was induced to consent through fraud (the deliberate misrepresentation of the effect of the consent) or duress (the exercise of undue pressure to obtain the consent) [Thompson et al. 1999]. Fraud and duress, however, are difficult to prove, and most birth parents lack the resources to pursue legal redress even when the violations of their rights are evident [personal communication with Dr. Diana Edwards, April 26, 2000]. Additionally in some states, even with proof of fraud or duress, revocation of a consent to adoption is permitted only if it is determined that revocation is in the child's "best interests" [Thompson et al. 1999]. In these states, courts commonly rely on the length of time that the child has been with the adoptive family as a factor in determining the child's "best interests" [Thompson et al. 1999], a standard that may reward efforts to "fight" the birth parents through protracted litigation and appeals [personal communication with Dr. Diana Edwards, April 26, 2000].

These issues raise a number of questions bearing on birth parents' consent. What is in a child's "best interests" when a birth parent's consent was induced through fraud or coercion? Does an adoptive placement—particularly when protracted as a result of litigation and appeals—overcome birth parents' interests when consent was not given in an informed manner? How does the resolution of these questions reflect societal values regarding the relative weight of birth parents,' adoptive parents,' and children's interests? These critical questions have not been closely examined and warrant greater attention.

Birth Fathers' Consent. The second set of consent-related issues in *Baby Jessica* centers on Dan Schmidt, the child's birth father. His lack of involvement in planning for his child was based not only on his lack of knowledge of the pregnancy but the fact that Ms. Clausen initially lied about the identity of the child's father. Only at the time of her own efforts to revoke her consent to the adoption did she correctly identify Mr. Schmidt as the child's father. These circumstances raise a host of issues related not only to Mr. Schmidt's rights—and his opportunity to demonstrate his interest in parenting his child—but the rights of other parties to the process, including the adoptive parents who relied on the birth mother's representations. What is the most effective approach to determining the rights of birth fathers who are excluded from the decision-making process? What options should be considered when the birth mother deliberately misidentifies the birth father?

Clearly, the failure of a birth mother to properly identify a known birth father presents an extremely troubling situation. A birth father also may be precluded from planning for his child, however, because an adoption agency advises the birth mother not to identify him. In a recent case in Canada, for example, a birth father was awarded custody of his daughter following her place-ment with an adoptive family 10 months previously [Zacharias 2000]. The birth mother stated that she had consented to the adoption after what she described as inordinate pressure by her own mother, who caused her to feel deeply ashamed about the pregnancy, and by a social worker at the adoption agency [Zacharias 2000]. The birth mother also testified that the social worker had discouraged her from identifying the birth father, warning that if she named him, he could block the adoption [Zacharias 2000].

Courts often have ruled in favor of birth fathers in cases in which the men were denied the opportunity to plan for their children. In a case that received the high level of media attention that *Baby Jessica* received, the court in *Baby Richard* [*In re Adoption of Doe* 1994/*In re Petition of Kirchner* 1995] ruled in favor of the birth father who was not informed by the birth mother of her pregnancy or her decision to place their child for adoption. Also as in *Baby Jessica*, the birth father immediately asserted his interests upon learning of his relationship to his child. Over a four-year period, he litigated his claims to the baby and ultimately, the Illinois Supreme Court ruled in his favor. In language to which some commentators have taken exception [Thompson et al. 1999], the court held that there was only one remedy for the lower courts' failure to vindicate "the real father": to take the baby from the "strangers" who had kept him "without right" and turn him over to the man who had a "preemptive right" to his child "without regard to the so-called best interests of the child" [*In re Adoption of Doe* 1994, p. 195].

The decisions in *Baby Richard* and *Baby Jessica* have been subject to great dispute, raising questions regarding the appropriate balancing of interests. Craig [1998, p. 413] cites those decisions with approval, noting that the birth fathers' successes in such cases stemmed from "the mothers' bad deeds, not the fathers' inaction." Craig [1998, p. 414, 416] supports judicial focus on the interests of birth fathers as opposed to a "best interests of the child" standard, arguing that "best interests of the child" is wholly subjective and deprives an unwed father of an opportunity interest before he even has the chance to pursue it. Craig [1998, p. 414-415] contends that the emphasis on "best interests" results from two factors: a focus on the mother's autonomy in making decisions during pregnancy, which Craig views as "a detriment to the rights of biological fathers;" and a growing tendency on the part of courts to rely implicitly and explicitly on personal beliefs about who should raise children—with greater value placed on adoptive parents because of financial advantage.

Hollinger [1995], on the other hand, raises questions about courts' emphasis on the rights of birth fathers in cases in which they come forward after an adoptive placement to claim the right to parent their children. She argues that greater attention should be given to the impact of a custodial change on the child and asks whether the dismissal of an adoption proceeding should result in the virtually automatic transfer of a child to a birth parent without taking into account the child's interests. Should the state be able to ignore the harm inflicted on the child by its own delayed procedures? If an adoption petition must be dismissed before it is granted, to whom should custody of the child be given? Hollinger advocates a policy that recognizes that depriving a child of family ties without consideration of the harm the child may suffer infringes on the child's rights. She writes that even a fit parent's claims to custody may be limited because of a child's independent right to remain in the only custodial environment she has known [Hollinger 1995]. Bartholet [1993b] also criticizes the judicial decisions in favor of birth fathers. She maintains that decisions in cases such as *Baby Jessica* are simply a "politically correct" approach that fails to consider the interests of children. Referring to the *Baby Jessica* case by the adoptive parents' name, she [1993b, p. A19] writes:

> The *DeBoer* decision threatens to create yet another barrier (to adoption), raising the specter that children may be removed months or years after placement simply because a previously unknown father appears on the scene.

No response to the quagmire of competing interests in such contested cases involving birth fathers has proven completely satisfactory. One approach has been state legislative action to create putative father registries which require unmarried birth fathers to comply with registration procedures in order to assert parental rights. Utah enacted such legislation in 1996, reasoning that:

> An unmarried mother, faced with the responsibility of making crucial decisions about the future of a newborn child, is entitled to privacy. She does not have an obligation to volunteer information with respect to the father [Utah Code Annotated 1996].

The legislature reasoned that when an unmarried man had a sexual relationship with a woman, he was on notice of the possibility of both pregnancy and placement of the child for adoption and, thus, could be required to register his parental interest [Utah Code Annotated 1996]. The UAA, by contrast, does not provide for a putative fathers' registry. Instead, it mandates a procedure that requires a diligent effort to identify and determine the whereabouts of a birth father so that he can be notified of the adoption proceeding and be given an opportunity to assert his parental rights in a timely manner. Hollinger [1999b, p. 2-50] writes that this approach protects "the mother's privacy interest in refusing to name the father" while at the same time requiring that "she be advised of the importance of naming [him]." She [1999b, p. 2-50] writes:

> The UAA attempts to balance the mother's desire to remain silent, especially if she has been the victim of the father's violence or emotional abuse, against the child's and the adoptive parents' need for information about the child's background.

The UAA, perhaps in direct response to *Baby Jessica*, also provides for legal action when a birth mother does not correctly identify the birth father. An action for fraud is permitted when the birth mother lies about the birth father's identity and the adoptive parent suffers a financial or emotional injury as a result. In addition, the UAA provides for civil penalties against a birth parent who intentionally misidentifies the other parent. It does not, however, penalize adoption agencies or adoption attorneys who discourage birth mothers from disclosing the identity of birth fathers. These parties may play equally powerful roles in foreclosing the opportunities of birth fathers to participate in planning for their children.

Practice Issues

The *Baby Jessica* and similar cases raise significant issues regarding the need for quality counseling for birth parents to promote fully informed decision-making regarding their children. Rosenberg [1992, p. 177] emphasizes that the crucial factors in a birth parent's decision to place her child for adoption are that she has the time to consider all options and she has the opportunity to make the decision based on her own judgment:

> We have become aware of the lifelong anguish felt by those who allowed themselves to make a decision based on others' judgments rather than their own.

To this end, Pavao [1998] emphasizes the need to counsel birth parents about the options that are available so that when adoption is decided upon, it is the right option for the parents and the child. She [1998] focuses on the importance of educating all parties to the adoption process before an adoptive placement is made. Melina and Roszia similarly highlight the importance of quality counseling for birth parents. They [1993, p. 126] write:

> It is particularly frightening to adoptive parents to have the birth mother contemplate her options. Adoptive parents can't imagine how the birth mother could resist the beautiful baby she is holding . . . Adoptive parents need to understand that if the birth parents have been getting good counseling and not operating in denial about the pregnancy, they have understood that their child would be beautiful and lovable and that they would want to parent him. They have understood that it would hurt to be separated from the child, but they know that they are not in a position to be effective parents. There's no reason to assume they will think differently now that the child is born and they can see the child face-to-face, but they still must have the opportunity to review that decision, if only so they can feel all the more confident about the placement.

Pavao [1998, p. 4] observes that although some birth parents are "predominantly clear" about the decision to relinquish, others are "extremely ambivalent about this choice." She [1998, p. 5] recommends, based on her work with birth parents, that:

> when a young birth mother is extremely ambivalent, it is invaluable to place her either with her own family, if they are available and supportive, or with a fostering family who will act as a holding environment for her while she parents the infant. Then she can make a fully informed and concrete decision whether or not to place her baby for adoption. . . . [This] give[s] the birth mother an opportunity to experience, concretely, what it is like to parent her baby seven days a week, twenty-four hours a day, and to make a decision concerning her own and her child's future that is based on reality, not on abstract thinking.

She [1998, p. 5] notes, however, that most adoptive parents and agencies fear that allowing such time will "mean fewer babies being placed for adoption" because birth parents, when given such an opportunity to consider the plan for their child, will decide to parent their children. She [1998, p. 5] contends, in response, that "when adoption is truly the plan of all parties involved, when it is done conscientiously and with compassion, it has a greater rate of lifelong success." She [1998, p. 5] concludes:

> There would be fewer contested adoptions and fewer situations of loss for preadoptive parents (who have already suffered enough loss) if we made sure that each and every adoption is truly the right decision.

International Adoption: The Impact of Adoption on Birth Parents

Extremely little attention has been given to the birth parents of children who are adopted internationally. International adoption by families in the United States began in earnest shortly after World War II and became a significant aspect of adoption in the

1990s—when both the number of children adopted internationally and the number of countries from which U.S. families adopted grew substantially. The relative recency of international adoption, the diverse cultures in which birth parents live, and the circumstances surrounding many international adoptions have limited the understanding of the adoption experience for birth parents in other countries.

To the extent that this issue has been examined, the focus has been on birth mothers and principally has addressed the circumstances surrounding their consent to the international adoption of their children. A number of investigations have responded to reports of pressures being brought to bear on poor women in developing countries to induce them to place their children for adoption. The United Nations has investigated international adoption practice in Guatemala, where there have been allegations that force was being used to convince women to place their children for adoption and that women were being deceived into consenting to adoption [UNICEF 2000]. In Honduras, claims have been made that young women were being paid to become pregnant, provided with healthy diets and prenatal care, and then expected to place their children for adoption [Pastor 1989]. In other developing countries, charges have been made that poor women were essentially functioning as surrogates for affluent families in Western countries [Neubauer 1988].

The limited research suggests that poverty and low social status typify the backgrounds of many women who place their children for adoption internationally. Pilotti's study [1993] of the demographic characteristics of Latin American birth mothers who consented to the international adoptions of their children, for example, found that economic and social disadvantage uniformly characterized their backgrounds. Birth mothers were found to be young—between the ages of 14 and 18; poor; unemployed or active in the informal sector as street vendors, beggars or prostitutes; poorly educated; and from neglectful or abusive home environments. Although some characterize the women who place their children for international adoption as simply lacking the capability to rear their children [see Bartholet 1996], any such incapacity, in reality, appears to be more closely associated with economic and social distress than with parenting ability or interest. Defence of Children International, an organization that has studied the intercountry adoptions of children from a number of developing countries, for example, concluded that "the vast majority [of birth parents] part with their children out of despair or with the hope to ensure the child's welfare or survival" [Lücker-Babel 1990, p. 2].

A review of the research and literature on the impact of adoption on birth parents in other countries reveals that little work has been done in this area. A study completed by Johnson and associates [1998] is one of the few efforts to understand the circumstances under which Chinese parents decide to abandon their children, thus making them available for international adoption. Of the 237 parents that the researchers interviewed, all but three were married and in their mid-to-late 20s and late 30s. The researchers found that in one-half of the cases, the decision to abandon the baby was made by the child's father, and in 40% of the cases, the couple made the decision together. In contrast to Pilotti's findings regarding birth mothers in Latin America, poverty did not appear to play a role in child abandonment in China [Johnson et al. 1998].

Cultural considerations were powerful factors in the birth parents' decisions, but the researchers found that pressures on families related to China's "one-child" policy varied by geographic location. Stricter adherence to the policy was found in suburban and urban areas, with the policy in rural counties found to be more of a "one-son-or-two-child" policy. Although considered a crime punishable by a heavy fine and sterilization of the mother, abandonment generally did not subject birth parents to such consequences. One quarter of the families reported that their actions were discovered, but they were not criminally prosecuted. The researchers observed:

> These punishments were in fact considered birth planning punishments, meted out for attempting to get away with over-quota births; in no case was abandonment treated as either a criminal or civil offense by virtue of

endangering or violating the rights of the child, or as a violation of the Marriage Law, which prohibits abandonment [Johnson et al. 1998, p. 480].

The researchers also found that couples generally abandoned infant girls who represented over-quota births rather than their only daughters. Only 11 of the 236 abandonments involved the parents' only girl and in each of these cases, the parents abandoned a daughter to preserve their chances for a son. In only a few cases had parents abandoned a boy, generally because the mother was unmarried; the child's father had died and the mother's new husband rejected the child; or the family already had a boy and wanted a girl [Johnson et al. 1998].

Although the researchers did not empirically measure the psychological impact of abandonment on Chinese birth parents (birth mothers, in particular), they found in their interviews that "birth mothers frequently expressed emotional pain and remorse for the act" [1998, p. 474], and "some birth mothers said they felt the loss of the child for many years, although most claimed to have gotten over it in time" [1998, p. 480]. One birth mother, who had abandoned her second daughter several years previously, explained that she "remained undecided as to whether she would ever proceed with another pregnancy despite the fact that she held a certificate of permission to give birth again (in hopes for a son) and was under great pressure from her husband and in-laws" [1998, p. 480].

The circumstances surrounding the decisions of Korean birth parents regarding international adoption also appear to involve cultural factors. During and immediately after the Korean War, Korean birth mothers who relinquished their children largely did so because the children were fathered by United Nations military personnel and, thus, were of mixed race and treated as outcasts by Korean society [Department of the Army Staff Communications Office, n.d.]. Mixed race births declined with the withdrawal of the American and British forces, but the stigma associated with out-of-wedlock birth remained, and full-blooded Korean children born to unmarried mothers also faced social stigma [Evan B.

Donaldson Adoption Institute 1999b]. Beginning in the 1960s, the majority of children adopted by families from abroad were full-blooded Korean children of unmarried mothers [Holt Children's Services 1999].

According to Molly Holt of Holt Korea [personal communication, March 2, 2000], one of the oldest adoption agencies in Korea, the typical Korean birth mother is very poor, from a very large family in which she is the youngest, and lacking in family and social support. In some situations, international adoptions result from family pressures on unmarried parents so they can marry the partners that their families have chosen for them [Holt, personal communication, March 2, 2000]. Nonetheless, the decision to relinquish a child for adoption is likely to carry high social costs for Korean birth mothers. Because the contraception of choice in Korea is abortion, proceeding with a pregnancy as a single woman brings social censure and involves a "sacrifice (of) many things— job, school, friends, and sometimes family" [Han 1999, p. 133]. Giving birth and relinquishing for adoption, though difficult, may be preferable, however, to choosing to parent a baby as a single woman, given the "overwhelming stigma of single motherhood and discrimination against children (who are) without legally recognized fathers" [Dorow 1999, p. 5].

One of the few resources offering counseling and support for single pregnant Korean women is Ae Ran Won, a home initially established for runaway girls, prostitutes, and "uneducated rural women migrating to the capital city in search of work" [Dorow 1999, p. 5; Ae Ran Won 2000, p. 2]. Counselors at Ae Ran Won report that about 85% of the birth mothers whom they serve choose adoption, and many prefer international adoption to domestic adoption by a Korean family. Dorow [1999, p. 35] explains that international adoption has become more attractive to Korean birth mothers because of the possibility of ongoing correspondence with their children and the opportunity to see them again, neither of which is possible with domestic adoption. Dorow [1999, p. 35] writes:

> An adopted person often is not accepted into Korean society, and may never know he or she was adopted. Not

only is adoption of a non-relative a new and strange concept for many Koreans, for whom blood ties are very important, but open adoption is nearly impossible. If a birth mother places her child domestically, in almost every case she will have no further contact with the child and adoptive family.

Because of the paucity of research, the psychological impact of adoption on Korean birth mothers is not well understood. Mrs. S. S. Han [personal communication March 2, 2000], who directs Ae Ran Won, has observed that birth mothers "often experience guilt, loss, and despair" about the decision to place their children for adoption. She further stated, however, that many women do not express regret for their decisions as they believe they had no other choice [personal communication, March 2, 2000]. Longer-term outcomes for birth mothers appear to vary: some women continue their education and marry; others seek employment after being terminated from their previous jobs because they were pregnant; and some are forced to drop out of school and are unable to return [Han, personal communication, March 2, 2000]. Mrs. Han [personal communication, March 2, 2000] indicated that only a few women choose to tell their husbands about their first babies.

As is the case with birth mothers in Korea, research on Japanese birth mothers is extremely limited. The characteristics of birth parents and the circumstances leading to their decisions in favor of international adoption must be extrapolated from the historical context in which the international adoptions of Japanese children occurred. An article printed in 1956 noted that as of 1952, there were approximately 4,000 "mixed blood" orphans in Japan and "about 600 of them were in welfare institutions of some kind. The rest were living with their Japanese mothers or other members of the girls' families—many in abject poverty" [International News Service 1956]. It was these children—most of whom were between 5 and 7 years old—who were adopted internationally in the 1950s [International News Service 1956]. These children were adopted primarily by American military families who had difficulty adopting domestically because agencies believed that their transient military lifestyles made them "poor parental risks" [Fleming 1956]. As the older ages of the children at the time of their adoptions imply, it was likely that significant social pressures led birth mothers to place their children for adoption internationally. Some birth mothers made the decision in favor of adoption once their children entered school and experienced harsh racial discrimination; other mothers placed their children for adoption because they were unable, on their own, to continue to support their children; and other mothers were forced to relinquish their children by their new husbands [International News Service 1956].

Even less is known about birth parents in Russia and Eastern Europe whose children are placed for adoption internationally. Birth parents in these countries, as in Latin America, are believed to face dire economic circumstances that make it extremely difficult for them to parent their children [Aronson 2000]. In other circumstances, birth parents may face significant personal problems—such as alcohol abuse [Aronson 2000]—that undermine their ability to parent. Much more remains to be understood about the psychological and social impact of adoption on Russian and Eastern European birth parents.

The Impact on Birth Parents of the Involuntary Termination of Parental Rights

In contrast to the fairly well developed body of the research that has explored the experiences of birth parents who themselves place their children for adoption, there has been little focus on birth parents whose rights are involuntarily terminated. Mason and Selman [1997, p. 2] noted that "the voice of the non-relinquishing parents has not been heard." There is consensus that the impact of involuntary termination of parental rights and adoption on parents "is a subject which merits further research," [Hughes & Logan 1993, p. 33], but the understanding of the experiences of this group of birth parents remains quite limited.

The few studies that have been conducted in this area—all of which are from Great Britain—are consistent in their findings of long-term psychological distress as a result of involuntary terminations of parental rights. Hughes and Logan [1993] identified two major characteristics of parents whose rights were involuntarily terminated: significant psychological problems and a continuing sense of anger and guilt that persisted long after their children were adopted. Mason and Selman [1997, p. 25], in their study of 21 birth parents whose children were placed with adoptive families after involuntary termination of parental rights, similarly found that adoption "had a devastating and long-term effect on the lives of most of the parents, leaving them with feelings of isolation and emptiness." Birth parents reported adverse effects on their mental and physical health and ongoing concerns about their children's whereabouts and well-being. Charlton and associates [1998], in their interviews with 65 birth parents whose rights were involuntarily terminated, also found that many birth parents suffered from significant and long-term health problems, which many parents related to mourning of their loss. The most commonly reported problems were physical symptoms associated with bereavement and trauma, such as sleeping problems, poor appetite, and dreams about either the loss of the child or about searching and the return of the child to them. The researchers also found that many birth parents described relationship difficulties, particularly with new partners. Some parents were reluctant to enter new relationships, and others felt a sense of isolation within relationships with individuals who had never known the children they lost.

Some commentators have suggested that parents whose rights are involuntarily terminated may be in a more protected position than parents who themselves make an adoption plan. Berry, Barth, and Needell [1996, p. 182], noting that "birth parents deserve to have their well-being considered and rights protected as they proceed through adoption," argue that "public agency adoptions seem to be best designed for these purposes because the birth parent has his or her own legal counsel." Mason and Selman [1997], however, found that the presence of legal counsel did not necessarily provide birth parents with strong protections or a sense of empowerment. In their study, birth parents reported difficulties obtaining quality legal representation, that is, attor-

neys who had experience in working with involuntary termination of parental rights cases and the ability to effectively present
such cases to the court. The court experience itself was traumatic
for many birth parents who described it as being "publicly branded
as bad parents" and as situations in which no one actually listened
to what they had to say [1997, p. 24]. Many parents also reported
that they felt "they were being painted as bad parents with little
opportunity to challenge this" [Mason & Selman 1997, p. 27].

Similarly, Charlton and colleagues [1998, p. 37] found in their
interviews that irrespective of the presence of legal counsel, birth
parents experienced the court process with a "sense of despair"
because "everything had already been decided." The judicial
process for birth parents "involve[d] not only loss of children, but
also a loss of self worth and confidence" [Charlton et al. 1998, p.
35]. The researchers [1998, p. 35, 39] noted:

> Many birth parents talked at length and in detail about
> attending court as a traumatic experience which resulted
> in feelings of humiliation and a sense of betrayal by the
> local authority which had previously been perceived as
> a helping agency...Many felt betrayed by social workers
> who had been perceived as helpers and suddenly became
> opponents in the legal battle. This shift from one of
> enabler and partner to adversary was the most difficult
> for birth parents to take in and contributed to their anger
> towards the social worker.

These findings are consistent with the research of Ryburn [1992,
p. 37] who found that legal proceedings—which birth parents
viewed as "very public declarations" of their unfitness—had a
significant psychological impact on birth parents. He found that
birth parents typically experienced long standing "anger, shame,
guilt and bitter recrimination" because of the process that led to
the termination of their rights [1992, p. 37].

The decision-making process by which efforts to reunify
parents and children are discontinued and involuntary terminations of parental rights are pursued has raised a number of
questions regarding the fairness and equity with which such

determinations are made. Littell [1997], for example, writes that decisions to involuntarily terminate parental rights can be undertaken fairly only when birth parents have not only the opportunity to develop parenting skills but also have access to needed resources—such as suitable housing, quality day care, appropriate health care, and an adequate family income. Wulczyn [1991] found that many communities lack such resources, and, as a result, children enter foster care in these communities at extremely high rates. Based on census tract mapping of the City of New York, for example, he found that high rates of poverty, infant mortality, and teen pregnancy clustered in resource-impoverished communities, and that in certain of these communities, more than 12% of all infants were placed in foster care before their first birthdays [Wulczyn 1991].

It is not clear to what extent children can be reunited with their parents when poverty and poverty-related problems such as homelessness precipitate foster care entry [Sherman 1989]. As a result of the Personal Responsibility and Work Opportunity Act [P.L. 104-193]—or welfare reform—and the Adoption and Safe Families Act [P.L. 105-89], it may be increasingly difficult to reunite children in foster care with their birth families. The Temporary Assistance to Needy Families program—which was created as part of welfare reform legislation—significantly limits the level of benefits and the time frame over which poor families may receive financial assistance [Freundlich 1997]. The Adoption and Safe Families Act requires more rapid processes to terminate parental rights, both when certain circumstances are present and when shortened time frames have been exhausted [42 USC § 671(a)(15)(D), 675(e)(4)(E)]. The combined effects of these federal welfare and adoption policies may well mean that more birth parents will face involuntary termination of parental rights or be encouraged to voluntarily relinquish their rights before an adversarial process is initiated [Freundlich 1999b].

Two service-related issues require consideration in the context of the current policy environment surrounding the involuntary termination of parental rights: the possible role of mediation in supporting birth parents' decision-making and the extent to which postplacement services for birth parents can provide support. Though in relatively early stages of development as a planning process, mediation has been used in some communities to facilitate cooperative planning between birth parents whose children are in foster care and the agencies that have legal responsibility for those children [Freundlich 1999a]. As a pioneer in the field of mediation in permanency planning for children in foster care, Etter [1993, p. 258] points out that planning for children in foster care presents a range of challenges, and she emphasizes that adoption as the plan for a child in foster care:

> arises by and large out of adversity. The painful social and personal conditions that make adoption necessary also make the parties to the adoption vulnerable. Ideally, the participants in any adoption will have their basic needs protected by the mediation process that also allows them to make choices that can work for the benefit of all.

In Etter's mediation program, services are provided to families in which involuntary termination of parental rights is likely to be pursued. Commenting on the benefits of mediation in these cases, Etter [1993, p. 258] notes that, "the mediator guides the process into a constructive problem-solving mode and helps parties to frame their proposals, consider their options, and approach other parties in a constructive manner." The *Fast Forward to Permanency* program in Houston, Texas, as distinct from Etter's program, offers mediation services across a range of case situations, including those in which a conflictual relationship has developed between a birth family and child protective services and is likely to affect their ability to work together cooperatively; cases in which the outcome—reunification with family or adoption—is not clear and options need to be fully explored; and cases in which a birth parent, because of mental impairment or other factors, needs assistance in navigating the child welfare system [Freundlich 1999a]. These programs suggest that third-party mediators can enhance birth parents' involvement in planning for their children and support their informed decision-making.

There has been little attention given to the services needed by birth parents after their rights have been involuntarily terminated and their children have been placed with adoptive families. Charlton and colleagues [1998, p. 94] found that the birth parents whom they interviewed "had very special needs which appeared not to be met by any agency." Mason and Selman [1997] similarly found that the significant needs of birth parents whose parental rights had been terminated involuntarily were not well met by agencies. Most of the birth parents they interviewed would not consider turning for assistance to the agency with whom they were involved and were hesitant about turning to *any* adoption agency. The "majority [of birth parents] said that it had been their families who stood by them and that without them, they would have had no one" [Mason & Selman 1997, p. 24].

Based on their research, Mason and Selman [1997] and Charlton and associates [1998] conclude that an independent support and referral body is needed to offer birth parents nonjudgmental services and assistance with the psychological impact of involuntary termination of parental rights. Charlton and colleagues [1998] offer a four-stage service framework to meet the needs of birth parents: witnessing—in which birth parents "tell their story" and the counselor acknowledges their experiences; impact—in which parents begin to absorb the impact of the loss of their children, including feelings of disbelief, disconnection, and anger; acknowledgment of the loss of the child—in which they deal with the realization of their changed role and identity; and living with the loss. They [1998, p. 79] specifically note that "birth parents rarely accept the loss of their child through adoption," and therefore, "the process of coming to terms with their loss is more about finding ways of living with it than about moving towards acceptance." One approach to such ongoing support—suggested by Harris and Whyte [1999]—is group services. Support groups, they [1999, p. 47] find, provide birth parents with important benefits, the "most obvious [being] that it allows them to meet and share with others who have experienced this type of loss, reduces their sense of isolation, and enables them to gain insight and understanding of their own situation."

The Impact of Adoption on Birth Parents: Openness in Adoption

Of growing importance in understanding the impact of adoption on birth parents is the trend toward greater openness, both in terms of birth parent involvement in planning for the adoption of their children and ongoing contact between birth and adoptive families following the adoptive placement. The impact of "open adoption," however, may be complex to assess because the term itself has been defined in a variety of ways. Sorosky, Baran, and Pannor [1984, p. 214], who introduced the concept of "open adoption," define it as:

> an adoption in which the birth parent meets the adoptive parents, relinquishes all legal, moral, and nurturing rights to the child, but retains the right to continuing contact and knowledge of the child's whereabouts and welfare.

Different interpretations of "open adoption," however, have developed since the seminal work of Sorosky, Baran, and Pannor, with resulting confusion about the concept [Gritter 1997]. Gritter [1997, p. 20] identifies four key elements of open adoption, which when taken together are consistent with the definition advanced by Sorosky, Baran, and Pannor, but which individually are sometimes referred to as "open adoption":

- the birth family selects the adoptive family,
- the families meet each other face-to-face,
- they exchange full identifying information, and
- they establish a significant, ongoing communication.

Romanchik [1999, p. 1] points out that although these elements represent aspects of open adoption, the critical feature is that "the adopted child has the potential of developing a one-on-one relationship with his or her birthfamily." She [1999] emphasizes that the birth parent-child relationship, rather than ongoing connections among the adults, is the hallmark of openness.

Nonetheless, it is important to note that the element of openness most broadly practiced is birth parent choice of the adoptive parent for her child [Yngvesson 1997]. Although a birth parent's level of choice varies significantly among adoption agencies and adoption practitioners, it is the aspect of openness that has been incorporated most readily into traditional adoption practice. As Yngvesson [1997] notes:

> [T]he "choosing" birth mother is easily incorporated into more familiar concepts of individualism and voluntarism, in ways that the visiting birth mothers, whose "choice" is not simply to identify the adoptive parents for her child but to become a part of their lives, is not.

Birth parent selection of adoptive parents has long been a key aspect of nonagency adoptions through independent attorneys as well as through wholly unmediated exchanges of a child between birth and adoptive parents [Modell 1994]. The integration of birth parent selection of adoptive parents into agency practice is newer and has been attributed to the pressures on agencies to transform the process in order to provide birth parents with greater power in "giving" their child to adoptive parents [see Modell 1994]. This significant change in agency practice is one in which agency social workers no longer, in Modell's words, "play God" [1994, p. 37] and birth parents instead make the decision as to who will adopt their child.

Some have suggested that having been given the opportunity to select the adoptive parents for their children, birth mothers now have greater power, if not primary control, in the adoption process [see Daly & Sobol 1994]. A recent news headline, for example, proclaimed, "Birth moms...understand that when a woman gives up a child for adoption, the control is all hers" [Belkin 1998]. Do birth parents—and, particularly, birth mothers—now have greater, if not ultimate, power and control in adoption? Romanchik [1997b] maintains that despite the opportunity to choose the adoptive parents for their children, birth parents continue to lack a meaningful level of control in the adoption process. Although she believes that greater openness empowers birth parents to an extent not usually possible in traditional, closed adoption and "when done right, birth parents are really given a voice in the outcome," she nonetheless argues that "total control is an illusion" [1997b, p. 2].

Lowe [1999] agrees with this assessment, arguing that birth mothers, despite greater opportunities to participate in the adoption process, remain subject to the prejudices of adoption professionals and prospective adoptive parents. She [1999, p. 31] writes:

> Would-be adopters and social workers alike have an image of the "typical" birth mother, and they look down on her in smug condescension. They think they are "rescuing" the poor confused dear, and expect her to be "grateful" to their charity in "saving" her child from a life that is not middle class, or a home that is not two parent. Even after decades of progress toward open adoption, birth mothers still pay. We pay every time someone tells us our child is so lucky to have found a good family (i.e., to be away from us). We pay when coworkers ask in disbelief, "How could you have given away your baby?"

Others emphasize that despite the empowerment that may accompany the ability to select the adoptive parents for their children, birth mothers face certain risks in pursuing this course [Rosenberg 1992]. Rosenberg [1992, p. 28], for example, writes that birth parents must:

> hope that agency home studies are valid or that private matchmakers are acting completely and in good faith...they can only hope that their (own) intuitions and judgments have been good ones. For the sake of their emotional well-being and the ability to go ahead with the relinquishment, they cannot afford to dwell on lurking concerns regarding the quality of adoptive homes and must repress images of any less-than-ideal circumstances.

In response to these concerns, B. Romanchik [personal communication, March 25, 2000] observes that when birth parents and adoptive parents are supported in choosing one another, fears about one another and issues of power and control are obviated.

Additional issues may be presented when birth parents faced with the prospect of an involuntary termination of parental rights are given the opportunity to choose or, at minimum, meet their children's adoptive parents. Chippindale-Bakker and Foster [1996] write that the opportunity to meet prospective adoptive parents may provide birth parents of children in foster care with greater power in the process. They [1996, p. 352] suggest that by "inviting biological parents to participate in the selection of the adoptive family, and then allowing these parties to meet," birth parents may be able to make decisions for their children with greater confidence. Although this approach may provide birth parents with a genuine role in planning for their children, Charlton and colleagues [1998] found in their study that obtaining birth parents' consent for adoption under such circumstances rarely provided genuine opportunities for open adoption. They [1998, p. 45] note:

> Consent is usually sought at a late stage when adoption is almost a *fait accompli;* the battle to secure the child's future by adoption has been essentially won, but for the birth parent the issue of having fought and lost remains. In these circumstances, being asked for consent seems to provoke primal instincts to protect the blood tie and the child from irreversible rejection or abandonment.

In relation to openness in adoption in the broader sense— in which birth and adoptive families exchange identifying information and establish a significant ongoing communication—many writers acknowledge that greater openness in adoption brings important benefits for birth parents but is not the "solution" to the losses they experience. Schaefer [1991, p. 293], for example, writes that "though the relinquishing mother has more leverage today than she did in my day (1965) and can often obtain some variety of 'open' adoption should she wish it, even open adoptions are not easy answers." Gritter [1997, p. 23] also warns against a view that "open adoption is an almost perfect solution to the problems of untimely pregnancy and infertility." He writes, "open adoption does not solve or fix either circumstance" [1997, p. 23]. Melina and Roszia [1993] similarly point to the realities of open adoption and emphasize that it is critical that birth parents understand:

> Open adoption means permanently terminating parental
> rights; having no legal rights to the child and perhaps no
> legal guarantee that contact with the child will be main-
> tained; forever giving up their role as parents to the child;
> realizing that the child's adoptive parents will probably
> raise the child differently from the way the birth parents
> would [1993, p. 41].

These realities of "genuine open adoption" provide the context for considering the impact of openness on birth parents.

Although the literature clearly identifies the challenges of open adoption [Gritter 1997; Melina & Roszia 1993], it also suggests that birth parents may benefit significantly from greater openness. Importantly, these benefits include the ability to have information about and some level of contact with their children [Melina & Roszia 1993]. Benefits also include the opportunity to resolve feelings of grief and deal directly with shame. Romanchik [1996], who has written extensively on the issue, observes that openness supports healthy grieving by birth parents. She notes that when there is a level of ongoing contact between birth parents and the adoptive family, loss is clearly before birth parents so that they are unable to deny the grief, a reality that may be painful but ultimately healing [Romanchik 1996]. Such contact requires birth parents to directly deal with their change in role—letting go of being a "parent" and becoming a "birth parent" and releasing any possibility of being the child's "mother" or "father" [Romanchik 1997a]. She also writes that open adoption encourages birth parents to confront the issue of shame because the "'dirty little secret' is replaced by the reality of a beautiful, innocent child" [Romanchik 1996, p. 7]. Speaking as a birth parent, Romanchik [1996, p. 7] writes:

> Shame gets driven out by our need to reaffirm our chil-
> dren and the relationship with their adoptive families.
> Our feelings of worth are then based on our part of the
> miracle of our children, instead of the opinions of others.

Several researchers have found that birth parents identify important benefits in greater openness in adoption [Fratter 1991;

Grotevant & McRoy 1997; Hughes 1995]. Fratter, for example, reported that birth parents found ongoing contact was a positive experience for themselves and for their children and their children's adoptive parents. Hughes [1995] found that birth parents wished to maintain a link between themselves and their children even when they were uncertain as to how such contact could be accomplished in their individual circumstances. Grotevant and McRoy [1997], in their comprehensive research on the impact of open adoption on all members of the triad, similarly found benefits for birth parents in greater openness. Specifically with regard to the impact of openness on birth mothers, they compared the experiences of birth mothers in fully disclosed adoptions (in which information was shared directly between birth parents and adoptive parents, usually through telephone calls and face-to-face meetings); confidential adoptions (in which no information was shared between birth and adoptive parents after the adoptive placement); and in mediated adoptions (in which information was exchanged between birth and adoptive families through an adoption agency staff member acting as an intermediary). They found that birth mothers in fully disclosed adoptions had higher levels of grief resolution regarding the adoption decision than did birth mothers who had no contact with the adoptive family or whose contact with the family had terminated. They also found that birth mothers in fully disclosed adoptions did not experience reduced levels of self-esteem and that self-esteem was essentially equivalent for birth mothers across all levels of openness.

Some, however, disagree with the assessment that birth parents benefit from open adoption. The view that open adoption is harmful to birth parents is reflected in various contributions to the National Council for Adoption's *Adoption Factbook III* [1999]. In one article, the perspective is advanced that openness—a "seriously flawed" concept advocated by individuals who "resemble the 'Flat Earth Society'" [Pierce 1999a, p. 238]—is not beneficial to any of the parties to adoption. In another article, the author argues—despite the findings from the research of Grotevant and McRoy—that open adoption is affirmatively harmful to a birth mother because she:

may not be able to fully grieve the loss of a child with whom she has continued contact. This may continually remind her of a painful situation and her emotional ties to the child, and lead to a prolonged period of unresolved grieving [Byrd 1999, p. 415].

In a third article, the author—who states that she is a birth mother writing under a pseudonym—describes her own experience with open adoption. The author states that the adoptive parents of her child agreed to have ongoing contact with her but then abruptly discontinued contact by sending her a formal, typed letter. She writes, in support of the adoptive parents' decision, that they put her "on the path to wholeness by standing by their own convictions" [Howe 1999, p. 340].

Objections to openness, however, have not consistently been based on concerns related to the potential for harm to birth parents. Pierce [1997], for example, argues that the risks associated with openness flow more from the intrusiveness of birth parents than from the harmful effects of openness on them. He [1997] portrays birth parents as "lurking about," eager to intrude into the lives of adoptees and adoptive families, selfishly pursuing their own needs irrespective of the effect of their conduct on others. Gritter [1997, p. 22] observes that such objections reflect concerns about birth parents' impact on the adoptive family, not considerations related to the well-being of birth parents. He notes [1997, p. 22]:

> Detractors like to portray a birthmother lurking in the attic, monitoring every conversation through the heat ducts, and waiting for the most inopportune time to make a dramatic and disapproving appearance. Against such a fantastic backdrop, the mundane reality—like a scheduled monthly dinner and a stroll in the park—seems rather tame. Critics routinely overlook the fact that birth families, just like adoptive families, want a measure of emotional distance.

One aspect of openness that the clinical literature has begun to address is the relationship between prospective birth parents and prospective adoptive parents prior to the adoptive placement and the extent to which such relationships present benefits and risks. Axness [1994, p. 5] writes that one of the "greatest dangers" in greater openness in preadoption relationships is that decisions will be made without "disinterested counseling." She [1994, pp. 5-6] explains that appropriate counseling:

> doesn't mean one or two sessions with a social worker for the birth mother, explaining her options and describing the process, highlighting the benefits to her in open adoption of being able to choose the adoptive parents. And it doesn't mean a coaching session for the prospective adoptive parents in techniques to help keep the birth mother from changing her mind. What it does mean, for the birth mother (or parents) is an exploration of the dizzying gamut of her feelings, a growing understanding of what the adoption plan will mean for her, her child, and the parents she chooses for her child, and preparation for the loss and grief that she will naturally feel if she chooses to go ahead with the adoption [1994, pp. 5-6].

Debate has surfaced as to when the relationship between prospective birth parents and prospective adoptive parents should begin. Betzen [cited in Axness 1999b] contends that the parties' intentions regarding their ongoing relationship should guide their contact in the preadoption period. He [cited in Axness 1999b, pp. 1-2] distinguishes between the intention to have a "semi-open" as opposed to a "fully open" adoption and writes that preadoption meetings between prospective birth and adoptive parents take on different meanings depending on the nature of the ongoing relationship. "Pre-birth meetings are probably the major manipulation technique used in the many semi-open, long distance adoptions that are happening every day in the US...Meeting an adoptive family is used by many to help manipulate toward adoption" [Betzen cited in Axness 1999b, pp. 1-2]. In these cases, birth parents may develop a sense of obligation to the prospective adoptive parents as a result of the interpersonal relationship or may become convinced that the prospective adoptive parents are clearly "better" than themselves [B. Romanchik, personal communication, March 25, 2000]. Additionally, as Diana Edwards has noted, the promise of ongoing contact—which may be expressly stated or, at least, generally implied from the preadoption relationship itself—may not reflect actual intentions; birth parents may be led to believe that there will be ongoing connections, which in reality never actually occur [personal communication, April 26, 2000]. In contrast to these situations, Betzen [cited in Axness 1999b] notes that when fully open adoption is intended, preadoption contacts may be in the interests of all parties. In these cases, "moments before birth in the meeting and getting to know each other are some of the most positive bonding experiences of a lifetime. They allow the birth and adoptive mothers to begin a long friendship" [Betzen cited in Axness 1999b, pp. 1–2].

Objections to contact between pregnant women and prospective adoptive parents, however, are not always based on the possible negative effects for birth parents. Cocozzelli [1989], for example, cautions against prospective birth parents meeting prospective adoptive parents because of the possibility of trauma to the adoptive parents if the birth parent decides to parent the child. He maintains that adoptive parents carry into the meeting with the birth parent "the expectation that they will adopt her infant" and if the mother changes her mind, this expectation will go unfulfilled. He comments that "in most fields of practice, this type of dramatic raising and lowering of clients' expectations would be considered unethical" [1989, p. 34], presumably viewing prospective adoptive parents as the principal clients. With a focus on the impact of decision-making on the prospective adoptive parents and not the birth mother, he urges efforts to "accurately predict the adoption decision of mothers so that potentially traumatic outcomes for adoptive parents can be avoided" [1989, p. 34]. This framing of the interests involved in contact between prospective birth and adoptive parents suggests the primary concern is the impact of openness on the adults involved. As discussed earlier, attention to the interests of the adopted person in relation to open kinship has been a missing element in consideration of these issues.

Summary

An understanding of the impact of adoption on birth parents requires an appreciation of the many psychological, social, legal, and political factors that shape their experiences. The very terms used to refer to birth parents and the decision-making process leading to adoption highlight the complexities inherent in this role and the value judgments of others regarding these triad members. Likewise, the historical context of infant adoption suggests that societal values other than respect for and concern about the interests of birth mothers and birth fathers have shaped practice in the past.

With regard to birth parents who place their children for adoption, research and the clinical literature offer some understanding of the dynamics associated with the decision-making process. Nonetheless, the conflicting findings regarding the impact of adoption on birth mothers—and to a far lesser degree on birth fathers—raises serious questions. How can the fairly homogeneous Australian research findings suggesting that birth mothers experience long-term negative psychological effects be reconciled with the large body of U.S. research suggesting highly positive outcomes? Are the differences attributable to differing value orientations that may shape the design and methodology of the respective studies? How can the dearth of attention to birth fathers be explained? To what extent do social attitudes about birth fathers account both for the lack of attention in the research and the intensely negative public reactions when birth fathers step forward to claim the opportunity to parent their children?

It is clear that relatively little is known about birth parents who may be considered nontraditional from the historical perspective: the birth parents of children placed for adoption internationally and the birth parents of children in the foster care system whose rights are terminated involuntarily. Anecdotal accounts suggest that birth parents in Latin American, Asian, and Eastern European countries resort to international adoption because of economic, personal, and cultural pressures, but the psychological and social impact of their decisions to allow their children to be adopted by families in other countries has not been studied. Somewhat more is known about the effects on birth parents of the involuntary termination of parental rights and the subsequent adoption of their children. The research suggests the importance of ongoing services because of the psychological impact of such proceedings but underscore the need for independent resources that birth parents can trust.

Finally, the trend toward greater openness may significantly effect the way in which adoption traditionally has impacted birth parents. Does the ability to select the adoptive parents for their children evidence greater respect for birth parents—with a consequent positive benefit for them in both the short and long-term? Does contact with the prospective adoptive parents during pregnancy promote birth parents' well-being or create serious psychological risks? Does ongoing contact after the adoption serve to promote resolution of grief and loss—as the research suggests—or further exacerbate those feelings—as commentators worry?

As birth parents become increasingly vocal and as greater openness provides additional opportunities for their voices to be heard, a better understanding of the impact of adoption on birth mothers and birth fathers may be possible. The relative invisibility of birth parents in the past has played a significant role in the development of adoption practice and policy for birth parents rather than by them. The extent to which this may change is unclear, given the persistence of conflicting societal values regarding the status of birth parents.

Part IV

The Impact of Adoption on Prospective Adoptive Parents, Adoptive Parents, and Adoptive Families

The issues related to the impact of adoption on prospective adoptive parents, adoptive parents, and adoptive families arise in large part because of the social and cultural context of parenthood in this country, a context that associates parenting with fertility and biological connections [Kirk 1984]. Because parenthood is seen as deriving largely from biological relationships, there are expectations that a "flesh and blood" connection will exist between parent and child; that there is the power to decide when one will become a parent; that bonding and attachment are the natural result of pregnancy and the birth process; and that children will resemble their parents to a greater or lesser degree [Daly 1992]. Achieving parenthood through adoption runs counter to these social and cultural expectations, whether adoption is sought following the experience of infertility or as the personal choice of an individual to build a family in a nonbiological way. The divergence between the general biological context for parenthood and the social context of adoptive parenthood sets the stage for consideration of a range of issues that impact those who seek to adopt and adults who form families through adoption.

This section first identifies the psychological and social processes involved in becoming an adoptive parent, processes that suggest certain vulnerabilities on the part of adopters that are essential to an understanding of the impact of adoption on these members of the triad. It then focuses on two areas in which the interests of adopters are particularly relevant: the social study and

129

legal processes involved in being "approved" as an adoptive parent and accorded adoptive parent status, and the decision-making processes involved in the selection of the child whom the adoptive parent will adopt. The impact of each of these processes on prospective adoptive parents is considered in relation to current and future practice and policy.

The Psychological and Social Processes Involved in Becoming an Adoptive Parent

An understanding of the impact of adoption on prospective adoptive parents and adoptive parents necessitates an appreciation of the psychological and social processes that characterize the experiences of adults as they strive to achieve adoptive parenthood. These processes take place in a sociocultural environment that may exacerbate the difficulties involved in psychologically and socially embracing parenthood through adoption. As a result, they provide a framework for considering a range of adoption practice and policy issues in the sections of this paper that follow.

The research and practice literature regarding the psychological and social implications of becoming an adoptive parent is extremely limited. The existing literature primarily focuses on the experiences of individuals as they determine that infertility will make pregnancy unlikely or impossible and opt to pursue parenthood through adoption. This emphasis is understandable given the fact that a majority of those seeking to adopt do so because of infertility-related problems. A recent study by Berry, Barth, and Needell [1996] revealed that most adopters have tried to become pregnant before adopting. The researchers found that 83% of those who adopted through private agencies, 80% of those who adopted independently, and 50% of those who adopted through public agencies had unsuccessful attempts at pregnancy. A large majority (86% of private agency adopters, 80% of independent adopters, and 49% of public agencies adopters) reported that they adopted because they were unable to have a biological child.

The literature makes clear that the transition from infertility to adoptive parenthood is a process fraught with uncertainties about the validity of parenthood achieved socially rather than biologically [Rosenberg 1992]. The difficulties associated with this transition are largely associated with social and cultural expectations of a biological basis for parenthood that emanate from pronatalist cultural values in American society [Daly 1992]. Pronatalism gives rise to assumptions that married couples will become parents [Daly 1992] and tends to characterize voluntarily childless couples as selfish because of their choice to forego children [Veevers 1980] and involuntarily childless couples as the objects of pity because of their inability to achieve the core expectation of parenthood [Daly 1988]. Hoffman-Riem [1989, p. 26] describes the transition from infertility to adoptive parenting as a process marked by "artificial construction" as opposed to the "normal parenting" that characterizes biological families. Infertility for many individuals triggers what she calls a "trajectory of denormalization" as the individual confronts the reality that biological parenthood may not be possible [Hoffman-Riem 1990, p. 3].

Infertility itself, a "major negative life event" [Abbey et al. 1992, p. 409], can have significant deleterious effects on the individual's well-being [Abbey et al. 1992] and can adversely affect the quality of married life [Ward 1998]. Infertility has been associated at the personal level with a diminished sense of self-esteem [Wright et al. 1991] and loss of a sense of internal control [Paulson et al. 1988], and at the interpersonal, or couple, level with a loss of a common dream [Burns 1987]; a sense of threat on the part of the partner who is infertile, knowing that the other partner could have a child [Humphrey 1986]; anger because childlessness has been forced upon the couple [Butler & Koralski 1990]; and loss of sexual self-esteem [Shapiro 1993]. Additional factors appear to come into play as individuals confronted with infertility begin to consider parenthood through adoption. This decision may come only after exhaustion of medically-assisted reproduction, which despite the costs, the personal indignities, and the uncertainties in terms of outcomes, may be vigorously pursued in order to have a child of one's "own" [Winter 1997]. Sandelowski [1995] describes feelings of unreality and inauthenticity on the part of individuals who begin the process of letting go of the potential for biological parenthood and considering parenthood through adoption. The key task for these individuals, she finds, is "assuming a parental identity" that varies from normative social and cultural expectations [1995, p. 127]. Kirk [1984] also focuses on identity issues associated with the transition from loss of the potential for biological parenthood to psychological acceptance of social parenthood through adoption. He writes that for adoptive parents to "get on with their lives with maximum effectiveness," they must achieve respect for "the dignity of their role while they understand and accept its reality" [1984, p. 49].

Sandelowski [1995] has described the experiential course of infertile couples who, having made the decision to adopt, move toward the point at which a child will be placed with them. She finds that this time period involves certain unique psychological processes that distinguish the achievement of social parenthood from that of biological parenthood. First, she finds that adopters strive to "create a temporal order" in order to cope with the unmarked adoption waiting period [1995, p. 129]. Because the waiting time to adopt contrasts markedly with the fairly well-defined period of pregnancy, adopters often attempt to gain control over the uncertainty and avoid "living only to wait for a child" [1995, p. 129]. Second, she describes a process through which many adopters "construct or reconstruct a family romance" for the child. These family romances tend to take the form of a biography for the child that meshes with the adopters' own biography and emphasizes that the child is "loved" by them [1995, p. 129]. Finally, adopters tend to "stake a claim" in order to "own" the child as their own [1995, p. 130]. This "claiming" process principally involves adopters' concerns about themselves as "genuine" parents: anxieties about being "accepted" as the child's "real parents"; efforts to de-emphasize "the importance of the blood tie between parent and child"; and struggles to establish a "right" to their child "by emphasizing the close biological or biographical match between them and their child" [1995, p. 130]. Sandelowski observes that many adopters, as a result of these concerns, feel "fully parental" only after they have a child for a longer period of time than the birth parents or foster parents had the child or after the adoption has been legally finalized [1995, p. 127].

In addition to describing the psychological processes associated with becoming an adoptive parent, the literature addresses the social processes of establishing adoptive parenthood. Daly [1992], in one of the few articles on the subject, focuses on resocialization as the model for this process. Resocialization involves relearning, that is "reorienting the already learned identity to a new set of circumstances" [1992, p. 399]. When applied to the process of becoming an adoptive parent, Daly suggests that resocialization involves identity evolution in which there are both continuous and discontinuous elements of the identity of "parent." The individual unlearns certain aspects of biological parenthood, not attainable in most cases because of infertility, and learns how to be a parent through adoption. From this perspective, parenthood is a core identity, and through resocialization, there is a shift from "having a child of one's own"—that is, a biological child—to "having a child." Enduring elements of the core "parent" identity remain while the individual lets go of certain aspects of biological parenting and develops new values, attitudes, and behaviors that shape the identity of "parent" into new adoptive form [1992, p. 405].

According to Daly [1992], resocialization also involves significant others with whom prospective adoptive parents come into contact and who are a part of the process through which they reconstruct their "new" identities as parents. When a couple seeks to adopt, their interaction is an essential aspect of resocialization as they work together toward an understanding of how each of them defines the meaning of parenthood, values the biological aspects of parenthood, and views adoptive parenthood, including expectations, concerns, and fantasies. Adopters also tend to "check out" the attitudes of others about their plans to adopt, including potential grandparents, other family members, and friends, and these responses feed into prospective adopters' own definitions of parenthood. Daly found that potential grandparents were particularly key to individuals' construction of their adoptive parenthood identity because of their relationship to the prospective adoptive parents and their interests in family continuity. She writes that parents of potential adopters also are involved in a resocialization process, reconstructing the picture they have in their own minds of their daughter or son as a "parent" and the picture they have of themselves as "grandparents" to the children of their children [Daly 1992].

It is important to note that infertility is not always an issue for prospective adopters, as the research of Berry, Barth, and Needell [1996] indicates. Among those who adopt from public agencies, and to a lesser extent among those who adopt through private agencies and independently, the decision to adopt often is not precipitated by unsuccessful attempts to become pregnant. Berry, Barth, and Needell found that half of the public agency adopters had not come to adoption because of an inability to have a biological child of their own, but because of religious or humanitarian reasons. For those adopters who have birth children of their own—a little more than half of public agency adopters, a fifth of private agency adopters, and a third of independent adopters [Berry et al. 1996]—the psychological and social stresses associated with infertility are not likely to be present. These individuals have met social and cultural expectations of biological parenthood and may not, as a result, struggle with self-doubts about their authenticity as parents.

A recurring theme in the literature regarding the psychological and social process of becoming an adoptive parent, irrespective of the role of infertility, is the concept of entitlement, that is, adoptive parents' "belief in their inalienable right and responsibility to act in ways that promote the adopted child's best interests" [Rycus et al. 1998, p. 900]. Mann [1998, p. 50] contends, at a sociocultural level, that adoptive parents struggle to feel entitled because society prizes biological parenthood as the ideal and "denies [to adoptive parents] the aspect of their unique role in the adoption narrative and fails to recognize the individuality of their story." At a more practical level, Rycus, Hughes, and Goodman [1998, p. 900] point out that many adoptive parents view their adopted child as "someone else's child" by virtue of the child's birth and history. This perception relates to adoptive parents' doubts about their "realness" as parents, either in general or in relation to a particular child. Questions about their parental "entitlement" may lead adoptive parents to doubt their ability to respond appropriately to the child and to tentative or inconsistent parenting—behaviors which, in turn, may create difficulties in managing the child's behavior and generate a high level of stress in the adoptive family.

Cohen and colleagues [1993], in their study of adoptive and biological children who presented for mental health treatment, found differences between adoptive and biological parents that they associated with parents' views of entitlement. They found that adoptive parents were more likely to attribute their children's problems to biological factors and early life experiences, while biological parents were more likely to cite current family factors as explanations for those difficulties. The researchers noted that although some biological families saw parental separation as a possible solution to the child's problems, adoptive parents were more likely to consider the removal of the child from the home as the potential answer, a resolution not suggested by any of the biological parents in the study [Cohen et al. 1993]. The researchers suggested that these findings might reflect feelings on the part of adoptive parents that they do not have the full right and responsibility to act on behalf of their child [Coyne et al. 1991]. The researchers, like Rycus, Hughes, and Goodman [1998] in their writing, noted that adoptive parents often fear alienating their child through the firm use of discipline and, as a result, develop more pessimistic views of their ability to gain control of the child's behavior [Cohen et al. 1993].

The psychological and social processes involved in becoming an adoptive parent, particularly for infertile individuals, reflect the vulnerabilities of prospective adoptive parents and adoptive parents in an environment that places value on biological parenthood. As noted by Brodzinsky, Smith, and Brodzinsky [1998], adopters face a range of tasks, including dealing with infertility in many cases, coming to the adoption decision, dealing with the anxieties associated with the adoption process, handling the social stigma of adoption, and developing the support of family and friends for the adoption. These processes provide a context for consideration of issues related to adoption policy and practice that have particular impact on prospective adoptive parents, adoptive parents, and adoptive families.

The Social Study and Legal Processes Involved in Being "Approved" as an Adoptive Parent and Accorded Adoptive Parent Status

Although some observers have described prospective adoptive parents as substantially different from traditional social service clients because they come to agencies "out of strength, volunteering for a highly desirable social role" and present themselves "in terms of well-being rather than incapacity" [Brown & Brieland 1975, p. 291], prospective adopters may not experience the administrative and legal process from this empowered perspective. Instead, the process of assessing prospective adoptive parents and determining their suitability to adopt—"the only screening for parenthood sanctioned in our society" [Lieberman 1998, p. 4]—may have a significant negative impact on individuals seeking to become parents through adoption.

Daly [1992] found in her work that the rigors of the procedures that individuals must undergo to become qualified to adopt heighten their sense of personal vulnerability. Mann [1998], likewise, has emphasized the sense of powerlessness that prospective adoptive parents may experience, which begins with their decision to adopt and then is accentuated by the processes leading to adoption. Clark, McWilliam, and Phillips [1998, p. 35] have described the assessment of prospective adoptive parents as a "daunting" experience involving a "passive and sometimes threatening process over which they had little control." Barker and colleagues [1998, p. 2] similarly characterize the assessment process as "an obstacle course" in which applicants must "jump through hoops," give the "right" answers to validate themselves as individuals and potential parents, and convince those with power—social workers within agencies—to allow them to parent. Summing up the impact of the assessment process, Boss [1992, pp. 26-

27] has noted that "if prospective adopters are not deterred by all these prospects [of the assessment process], we may rest assured that they would have to be amongst the most stout hearted, resolute, patient, and persistent people . . ." These observations suggest a range of concerns related to the extent to which the assessment process evidences respect for prospective adopters and acknowledges their integrity as individuals. Questions are also raised regarding the appropriate nature and scope of the process of assessing the suitability of prospective adoptive parents. Does the process ensure fair consideration based on clear standards of assessment? Or, is it far more arbitrary?

The assessment or "home study" process used by public and private adoption agencies has been described in a variety of ways, including:

> A set of organizational criteria for being a good adoptive parent...used as a screening for determining how well couples match up with the organizational expectation for what an adoptive parent should be [Daly 1992, p. 411].

> The screening of applicants to identify those most suited for the role of adoptive parents...[focusing on] predicting the applicants' capacity for parenthood, with this assessment ideally projected to cover the twenty years the child will be dependent [Brown & Brieland 1975, p. 291].

> The process...lead[ing] to the final decision as to whether the agency will recommend placement of a child with the applicants and if so, the type of child for whom the applicants would be an adoptive resource [Child Welfare League of America 2000, p. 57].

It is often, in the words of Kirk [1984, p. 40], "the professional outlook" that frames the determination of an individual's eligibility for adoptive parent status. In a more critical tone, Hollinger [in press. p. 3] refers to the "powerful and opinionated cast of workers, lawyers, counselors, and other members of the 'helping professionals'" who are enlisted to "scrutinize" and "evaluate" prospective adoptive parents' suitability. This process, with "the circumstance of [the agency] having power over applicants" [Kirk 1984, p. 40], raises issues related to the philosophy that may underlie the adoptive applicant assessment process and the specific strategies utilized to reach a determination of the suitability of the individual applicant.

Issues related to the underlying philosophy of the assessment process focus on the extent to which the process may strive to identify the "perfect" adoptive parent. The search for the ideal in adoptive parents may be based on a concern that an incorrect determination could result in serious harm. Brown and Brieland [1975] point out that the assessment process may lead to two types of errors, the rejection of suitable applicants and the acceptance of unsuitable ones, with the second error viewed as far more serious because of its implications for the welfare of children. This concern may prompt the use of assessment in a way that perpetuates the "superfamily" myth [Rycus et al. 1998, p. 891]. Alternatively, the search for the "superfamily" may be an extension of a process that has its roots in a historical tradition of professional determinations as to who is a "deserving" adoptive parent.

As Gill [in press] relates, the search for the ideal adoptive parent has historical roots dating back to the 1930s and 1940s. At the turn of the century, the primary emphasis in social services, as limited as they were, was on prevention of harm to children. As the practice of child welfare grew and evolved over the succeeding decades and adoption became a more significant service, however, the role of the professional likewise changed. By the 1940s, the professional responsibility of adoption social workers had been redefined from that of screening out inappropriate prospective adoptive parents to "creat[ing] only the 'best' adoptive families," that is, families judged to be the "most normal" [Gill, in press, p. 3]. Although some social workers believed that normality was "hard to define, yet easy to feel and see" [Hutchinson 1943, cited in Gill, in press, p. 8], most adoption practitioners endeavored to describe with some specificity what "normal" meant for adoptive families. "Normality" generally was associated with the features of the biological family, but for purposes of determining individual applicants' suitability, "normality" required that applicants "fit" within a "psychological model defined by social workers" [Gill, in press, p. 11]. Applicants were required to have "normal" parental motives, be of "normal" age and fulfill "normal" gender roles. From the 1940s through the mid-1960s, individuals deemed to be deserving to adopt revealed appropriate "unconscious motivation for adoption of a baby," largely based on a desire to parent that had been thwarted by organically-based infertility; were of youthful age [not older than the mid-30s]; were married; and accepted traditional gender roles, which was seen as a "sign of 'emotional security' in applicants for parenthood" [Gill, in press, pp. 11-12]. Divorced status or homosexuality was anathema. As Gill [in press, p. 16] concludes, up to 1965, "applicants that did not fit the agencies' profile of ideal parents—such as career women, couples over 40, single applicants, and gays and lesbians, for example—were excluded without much difficulty."

Remnants of this historical search for the "perfect" adoptive parent may persist in contemporary practice. In more modern terms, assessments of prospective adoptive parents may be undertaken through "an ethnocentric lens" in which any aspect of the prospective adopter that is "different" is considered "deviant" and potentially harmful to children [Rycus et al. 1998, p. 891]. There may be little understanding of a family's cultural context, and, as a consequence, strengths may go unrecognized, and the family's structure and organization, values, and coping style may be viewed as "dysfunctional" [Rycus et al. 1998, p. 891]. Current debates regarding the appropriateness of allowing gay and lesbian individuals to adopt [Smothers 1997; Verhovek 1997] may reflect a continuing belief in the concept of "normality"—as defined in terms of the traditional nuclear family—in relation to who should adopt. Similarly, prospective adoptive parents with physical disabilities may find their suitability to adopt closely scrutinized, even in cases in which the individual has raised biological children [see *Adams v. Monroe County* 1998]. According to Barker and colleagues [1998], adoption agencies and social workers retain considerable power. Agencies may exercise this power through assessment processes that tie determinations of adoptive applicants' suitability to a range of prospective adoptive parent characteristics—including race, religion, culture, class, disability, and sexual orientation—and individual social workers may exercise power through basing assessment decisions on their own values or subjective beliefs [Barker et al. 1998].

Despite what may be a general sense that adoption agencies "know" who is a suitable adoptive parent, neither practice nor literature provides a well-articulated set of criteria that agencies use or should use in determining whether an individual will be a "good" adoptive parent. The most comprehensive work has been done by Rycus, Hughes, and Goodman [1998, pp. 892-902] in their delineation of criteria for the assessment of adoptive families for children with special needs. In their framework, two categories of criteria are utilized: traits and characteristics that enable a family to parent a child with special needs without incurring undue family stress, and traits and characteristics that are essential to meeting the child's special needs and promoting the child's healthy development. These characteristics, which may be difficult to definitively measure, encompass parents' expectations for adoption, personal maturity, the stability and quality of the individual's interpersonal relationships, resilience and coping skills, parenting skills, empathy, a "hands on" parenting style that engages the child, and the capacity to make a "lifelong" commitment to a child.

There is even less guidance in the literature regarding the evaluative criteria that private domestic and international adoption agencies should use to evaluate prospective adoptive parents for infants and young children in this country or from abroad. To the extent that assessment criteria are identified, they tend to be global in nature and, according to some commentators, of questionable value in attempting to determine the suitability of an applicant as a parent. Kirk [1985], for example, found in his review of agency selection approaches that agencies tended to use criteria based on psychodynamic theory, including the "emotional health" of the applicant assessed on the basis of the quality of the relationship between the prospective adoptive couple and between the couple and their own parents and siblings. Kirk questions the validity of such criteria defined in psychodynamic terms, asking how such information could assist a social worker in predicting how an individual will "act *as parent* in the changing circumstances of the family cycle years later" [Kirk 1985, p. 91 (emphasis in original)].

The absence of clearly defined criteria for selection of adoptive parents and the difficulties in actually assessing applicants based on the criteria that have been suggested leads to the question whether current assessment processes might, as an alternative, appropriately and clearly define criteria indicating who should not adopt. Are there characteristics or current or past behaviors that should be used to automatically exclude individuals from adopting, irrespective of their desire to do so? Would clarification and communication of exclusionary criteria at the outset of the assessment process result in a process that reflects greater respect for and a better appreciation of the interests of prospective adoptive parents?

Although the literature addresses this issue to some extent and there has been at least one broad attempt to define such criteria and their proper use by statute, it does not appear that the current use of exclusionary criteria significantly clarifies the decision-making process. Rycus, Hughes, and Goodman [1998, pp. 902-904], in one of the best efforts to address this issue, suggest that individuals should not be permitted to adopt when there is documented or very strongly suspected history of sexual abuse or the existence of a sexual control or conduct disorder; current abuse of or addiction to alcohol or other drugs; and severe mental illness or emotional disorder. Beyond these criteria, however, they indicate that less serious but nonetheless significant problems should prompt an individualized assessment to determine whether an individual can appropriately and safely parent a child, including:

- a history of child abuse or neglect

- a history of arrest and/or felony conviction

- a history of domestic violence

- previous substance abuse or mental health problems

- personal issues related to the individual's own child-hood victimization

- significant problems parenting their biological children

- significant interpersonal problems

As their analysis suggests, they find that few criteria constitute a basis for absolute exclusion, and they give considerable latitude to agencies to make determinations of individual applicant's suit-ability in light of significant problems. This approach highlights the importance of an individualized approach to consideration of applicants' suitability, while at the same time acknowledging that adults with certain conditions or past or current behaviors present too much of a risk to a child placed with them through adoption.

In a different approach, the Uniform Adoption Act (UAA) makes clear that no criterion should pose an absolute barrier to the opportunity to adopt, but that instead certain characteristics or behaviors, when assessed on an individualized basis, may serve to exclude an individual from adopting. The criteria listed by the UAA include physical and mental health problems, including any history of abuse of alcohol or drugs; whether the individual has been charged with domestic violence or a violation of the state's child protection statute; whether the individual has been con-victed of a crime other than a minor traffic violation; and "any other fact or circumstance that may be relevant in determining whether the individual is suited to be an adoptive parent, includ-ing the quality of the environment in the individual's home and the functioning of other children in the individual's household" [Uniform Adoption Act, § 2-203]. The UAA's approach tends to place weight on furthering the ability of adults to adopt. It limits the bases for exclusion to "*specific* concerns that pose *significant risks of harm* to the physical or psychological well-being of the minor" [Uniform Adoption Act, Comment to §2-204 (emphasis added)] and provides adults who receive an unfavorable evalua-tion with the opportunity to petition a court for review of the evaluation and obtain a judicial determination that he or she should be permitted to adopt [Uniform Adoption Act § 2-206].

There are issues warranting consideration in both an approach that provides agencies with wide latitude to accept or reject an adoptive applicant and an approach that, in effect, provides adults with a broad entitlement to adopt. With regard to discretionary approaches by agencies in determining the suitability of adoptive applicants, the issue is one of inherent fairness to adoptive applicants in relation to the validity and reliability of the decision-making process that leads to acceptance or rejection. Brown and Brieland [1975], in their early work and one of the few studies on this issue, examined the processes that agencies used in evaluating couples who sought to adopt infants. They reported the results of two nationwide studies of 184 social workers from 27 adoption agencies in which social workers indicated, based on the criteria they generally utilized in their own practice, whether they would accept or reject certain prospective adoptive couples. The researchers found that there was a statistically significant level of agreement among the social workers in their judgments, but they emphasized that from a practical standpoint, the level of agreement was not "high enough" [1975, p. 293]. They found that within many agencies, social workers were evenly split as to whether a particular applicant couple should be accepted or rejected, suggesting that social workers' judgments of the applicants' strengths and weaknesses were based on widely different value systems.

In the researchers' follow-up study of social workers' assessments in 13 agencies in the Chicago area, statistically significant levels of agreement regarding whether to accept or reject 5 hypothetical couples was found, but again there was considerable disparity among social workers from the same agency in their assessments of the couples. The researchers found that the ratings for one hypothetical couple presented to the social workers indicated that the couple had an almost even chance of being accepted or rejected depending on the social worker who evaluated them, leading the researchers to observe with consternation that "no applicant expects to be rejected because he saw the wrong worker" [Brown & Brieland 1975, p. 292]. With this concern in mind, the authors highlighted the need to identify criteria essen-

tial to assessment decisions and to utilize standardized procedures to obtain and give weight to the most relevant data. They
urged practice changes to ensure that "screening would . . . become
less of a hunting expedition" [1975, p. 295]. They also expressed
concerns about the length of the assessment process, particularly
when it was apparent early in the process that the outcome would
be unfavorable for the applicant.

Studies like those of Brown and Brieland as well as informal
observations of agency assessment processes have led a number of
commentators to question whether a legitimate basis for assessment of adoptive applicant exists and, if it does not, whether
prospective adoptive parents are being subjected to an inequitable
process for which agencies have little accountability. McKenna
[1989] takes issue with agency decisions about who will be a good
adoptive parent, pointing to the highly subjective nature of the
assessment process, which he believes is rife with problems.
Ryburn [1991, pp. 20-21] likewise observes that:

> Social work notions of assessment are based on the idea
> that there is an objective reality concerning those whom
> we assess, and that through a process of careful enquiry
> we can come to discover what this reality is. Such a belief
> in my opinion accords to recruitment and placement in
> adoption a scientific base that is very far removed from
> the "hit and miss" process which I think it really is.

There have been no outcome studies evaluating different methods
of assessing adoptive parents either in terms of their effectiveness
in recruiting adoptive families or achieving optimal outcomes for
children [Sellick & Thoburn 1996]. There is some evidence from
nonclinical studies that adoptive parents tend to demonstrate
good psychological health and levels of marital adjustment at the
time of adoption [Levy-Shiff et al. 1990]—an outcome that might
be associated with quality assessments of personal, marital, and
family stability. It is unclear, however, whether this evidence
supports current assessment processes or suggests that individuals who seek to adopt, through a self-selection process, tend to
have certain personal and social strengths.

An alternative to the discretionary assessment process utilized by agencies is a process that essentially assumes the suitability of all adoptive applicants, barring only the very few who are determined to be patently unfit because of criminality or extreme mental health problems [Martin 1988]. Such an approach could conceivably be viewed as consistent with the interests of those who seek to adopt by providing them with the power to achieve adoptive parenthood with few, if any, barriers to accomplishing that life goal. Even those who vociferously criticize the current assessment system, however, maintain that there is a need to exclude certain prospective adopters, and they do not endorse a virtually unregulated system. Bartholet [1993a, p. 78], for example, while advocating an approach in which "all who want to become adoptive parents would be presumed fit," nevertheless proposes a licensing system to disqualify individuals with past histories of serious or persistent substance abuse or prior child abuse or who are unable to meet a child's basic needs because of serious ill health, advanced age, or other reasons. Her rationale for disqualifying certain adults from adopting is to "assure people that adoption would not result in the kinds of abuses that occurred in the nineteenth century" [1993a, p. 78].

Another approach to assessment of prospective adopters is presented by those writers who have advocated greater power sharing with prospective adoptive parents, an approach that may best balance the interests of individuals seeking to adopt with the needs and interests of children. Clark, McWilliam, and Phillips [1998, p. 36] write that the "power of assessment and evaluation" should be "handed back" to prospective adoptive parents as much as possible. They and others [Stevenson 1991; MacFadyen 1995] emphasize that this shift is more likely to occur if the emphasis moves away from social workers' professional assessment of families to self-assessment by prospective adoptive parents. Similarly, Barker and colleagues [1998, p. 2] advocate the use of self-assessment by prospective adoptive parents, particularly regarding the adoption of children with traumatic histories. They emphasize that the key issues should be how applicants can be prepared effectively "to learn about what is involved [in the adoption of children with special needs], to reflect honestly and realistically on their capacity to parent such children, to engage in mutual and genuinely constructive dialogue regarding their strengths and needs, and to work with a range of supportive networks." They acknowledge agencies' professional responsibility for assessment but insist that it should be carried out fairly and sensitively, within acceptable time frames, and according to clearly defined criteria and standards.

In addition to the social assessment process and its impact on prospective adoptive parents are the legal processes required to complete an adoption and the inherent uncertainties associated with finalization. The literature has not addressed the impact of legal processes on prospective adoptive parents to any significant extent, although anecdotal accounts abound regarding the stresses of the "legalities" of adoption. The waiting period for legal finalization—which may range from several months to a year or more depending on the jurisdiction and the type of adoption—is often identified as a source of anxiety for prospective adoptive parents. It presents the possibility that, even having been "chosen" and a child placed with them, prospective adopters will not achieve parenthood.

Stresses related to the legality of birth parents' consent to the adoption arise in two situations. When birth parents change their minds about the adoption plan after initially planning a placement with an adoptive family, the prospective adoptive parents may experience significant stress and grief [Rosenberg 1992]. Even more intense emotional distress may be experienced when the child has been placed with the adoptive family and one or both birth parents come forward to claim the return of their child to them [Brazelton 1989]. Although such situations are rare, media focus on contested adoption cases such as *Baby Jessica, Baby Richard*, and *Baby Emily* has tended to imply that adoptive placements are routinely subject to litigation initiated by birth parents who seek to reclaim custody of their children—thereby exacerbating the anxieties of many prospective adoptive parents. The uncertainties inherent in waiting and the misperception that adoptions are frequently contested may explain Sandelowski's

[1995] finding that many adoptive parents do not feel truly parental until the adoption is legally finalized.

Other aspects of the legal process may accentuate the stresses on prospective adoptive parents and undermine the sense that parenthood can be achieved predictably through adoption. Of particular concern to prospective adoptive parents are the administrative and bureaucratic issues related to the interstate adoptive placements of children and the complexities involved in intercountry adoption, immigration, and naturalization [Gelber 1999; Wendell & Rosenbaum 1999]. These additional layers of legal processes, reflecting the complex jurisdictional aspects of adoption, may add to what prospective adoptive parents already perceive as a "legal gauntlet." The research and literature has not addressed these issues to any extent. The overlay of the legal processes on the social processes involved in qualifying to adopt and achieving parenthood through adoption, however, warrants attention.

The range of issues related to the social study and legal processes involved in the approval of adoptive parents and the conferring of parenthood status highlight the extent to which prospective adoptive parents may be significantly affected by the adoption process. At the social study level, there are a number of questions: Does self-assessment, compared to the prevailing professional approach to determinations of suitability to adopt, better reflect respect for prospective adoptive parents? Or do other approaches more appropriately balance the interests of adults who seek to adopt and the interests of children whom they adopt? With regard to the legalities of adoption, other questions arise: To what extent do the legal processes related to adoptive placements and adoption finalization further subject prospective adoptive parents to stress? Do the "legalities" of adoption serve to further undermine prospective adoptive parents' sense of well-being or are they necessary safeguards that ensure the protection of all parties' interests?

The social and legal context of achieving adoptive parenthood may suggest a high level of vulnerability and limited autonomy on the part of prospective adoptive parents. Other realities, however, regarding the position of prospective adoptive parents in relation to other members of the triad and vis-à-vis adoption agencies must be considered. Developments suggesting greater recognition of the rights and interests of prospective adoptive parents provide an important counterpoint to concerns about the vulnerabilities of prospective adoptive parents.

Issues Related to Adoptive Parents' Right to Adopt and Decisions to Adopt Particular Children

One recurrent issue in adoption is the extent to which adults have a "right," in any sense of the term, to adopt. The issue of the right to adopt is one that goes to the meaning of adoption as a service. Is adoption first and foremost for children who need families or for adults who wish to parent? While it can be argued that adoption can accommodate the needs of both children and adults and perhaps in many, if not most, instances does so, the primacy of adult needs is often implied by those who maintain that adoption is the equivalent of biological parenthood [see Bartholet 1993a], and, consequently, contend that it should be structured to mirror the wholly unregulated achievement of parenthood through biological means. From this perspective, it could be argued that an adult should have the opportunity to adopt if he or she wishes to do so, unfettered by any processes that create barriers to the achievement of the desired identity of "parent."

On the other hand, there are those who express concerns that such an emphasis on adults having the opportunity to adopt may not only reinforce the prevailing emphasis on adult interests—as opposed to an emphasis on the needs of children—but may create an environment in adoption that is even more harmful for children [Hirst 1997]. What weight should be given to prospective adoptive parents' interests in becoming a parent through adoption? Specifically, to what extent is any adult's interest in adopting stronger than the interests of a child in being placed with an adoptive family that meets that child's specific needs?

The processes involved in bringing together prospective adoptive parents and a child—often referred to as "matching"—are complex. The nature of "matching" has varied over time and has taken different meanings in the context of different types of adoption. For decades, "matching" referred to efforts, particularly in the adoptions of infants, to select a family for a child or, perhaps more accurately, a child for a family based, at least to some extent, on physical similarity [Gill in press; McRoy & Zurcher 1983]. In the area of special needs adoption, "matching" generally has referred to attempts to identify a family for a child based on an understanding of the child's emotional needs and the strengths that a particular family brings in responding to those needs [Veevers 1991]. A range of practice issues in the "matching" of children and families has been identified [McRoy 1999], but in relation to decision-making by adoptive parents, the key considerations appear to be the extent to which adoptive parents have or should have the "right" to adopt a child of their particular specifications—thereby defining the "match" they desire; and the extent to which adoptive parents are given the opportunity to make a fully informed decision about adopting a particular child—thereby sanctioning the "match" as one that they are prepared to undertake.

Parental Rights to Adopt a Particular Type of Child

A corollary to the position that adults have a right or near-right to adopt is that prospective adopters are entitled to select the specific type of child whom they wish to adopt—based on such factors as age, physical characteristics, race, or other characteristics. As the supply of healthy Caucasian infants available for adoption has diminished, there has been a widening disparity between the aspirations of would-be adopters in terms of the children they wish to adopt and the characteristics of children who typically need adoptive families [Phillips 1998]. Market forces have become increasingly powerful as adults seek opportunities to adopt children of preferable racial or ethnic backgrounds, health status, or other defined characteristics. Just as some prospective parents sought—as was stated more unabashedly in the 1950s—a "blue ribbon" baby, the current pursuit of a "designer" or "perfect" child is now taking place through assisted reproductive technology and through adoption. Prospective parents' willingness to pay greatly inflated sums for eggs donated by women with highly desirable physical and intellectual characteristics [see Kolata 1999] parallels the willingness of some prospective adoptive parents to pay inflated adoption "fees" for a healthy, Caucasian infant. Increasingly, the ability to expend maximum resources translates into the realization of adults' desires for a specific type of child. In the adoption context, does the ability to obtain a child who has preferable characteristics serve to reinforce the notion that adults have rights to adopt certain children?

Recent legal developments suggest that there is increasing acceptance of the view that adults have the right to adopt children with certain characteristics, with very young age and good health being the most desirable features. As the demand of prospective Caucasian adopters has outstripped the number of healthy Caucasian infants available for adoption, Caucasian adopters' interest in healthy infants of color, notably biracial and African American infants, has increased [Chandra et al. 1999; Howe 2000]. Bartholet [1993a, p. 113], addressing this issue, writes:

> You have only to step into the world of adoption to realize that it is largely peopled by prospective adoptive parents in search of white children…Many white adopters start the adoption process with no apparent racial preferences. Many others begin their quest thinking of a white child and turn to transracial adoption after considering their options. For them, transracial adoption may appear to be a second choice. But the fact is that for a very large number of adoptive parents, adoption itself is a second choice, forced upon them by their inability to reproduce. It is understandable that when they first contemplate adoption, they would be interested in finding a biologic and therefore a racial look-alike…The evidence…indicates that when whites arrive at the point of consciously choosing to enter parenting relationships with black children, the relationships work.

Her analysis suggests that although Caucasian adopters prefer to adopt Caucasian children, they—upon realizing the current demographics of adoption—are willing to "settle" for a child of color. Her argument goes further, however, and contends that Caucasian adopters should not only be given a full opportunity to adopt children of color, but have a right to do so [Bartholet 1993a].

Bartholet's argument rests on the autonomy interests of prospective adoptive parents [1998]. Unlike Banks [1998]—who argues that the government should not allow prospective adopters to express any preference regarding the racial background of the children whom they will adopt—she believes that autonomy interests support adopters' private preferences regarding the race of any child they would adopt [Bartholet 1998]. She also maintains, however, that the right to hold a "private preference" about the race of the to-be-adopted child extends to a right to have that preference realized. She and others [see Kennedy 1994] rely heavily on federal law to ensure the realization of Caucasian adopters' interests in adopting children of color.

The 1996 amendments [Small Business Protection Act, P.L. 104-188, Section 1808] to the Multi-Ethnic Placement Act [P.L. 103-382] (collectively, "MEPA"), resulted in a prohibition on the consideration of the race, color, or national origin of prospective foster parents, adoptive parents, or children in making foster care or adoptive placements. Although the argument is made that these provisions are child focused and designed to facilitate the adoptive placements of children of color in foster care [Brodzinsky et al. 1998], the enforcement provisions of the law [P.L. 104-188] and the implementing regulations [Federal Register 2000] suggest that a principal goal is to give adults the full opportunity to adopt without racial or ethnic considerations impacting their ability to adopt a child of their choosing. The implementing regulations for MEPA, for example, provide that the Office of Civil Rights conduct an immediate investigation upon receipt of any "letter of complaint" describing a "potential violation" of the law [Federal Register 1998]. It seems likely—given the general demographics of prospective adopters and waiting children in foster care [Chapin Hall Center for Children 1997; Tatara 1993] and the nature of most publicized disputes in this area [see Lehmann 1999]—that such complaints will be filed by Caucasian adults denied the opportunity to adopt a child of color rather than by children (through their legal representatives) denied the opportunity to be adopted without delay.

In a similar vein, other laws are being relied upon increasingly by prospective adoptive parents to assert claims of discrimination when they are not approved to adopt or have been approved to adopt but a child has not been placed with them. Claims have been brought under federal law (such as the Americans with Disabilities Act) and state human rights laws alleging discrimination on the basis of religion. Claims by prospective adoptive parents under antidiscrimination laws based on race, disability, and human rights can be viewed as promoting adult rights to adopt— either in general or to adopt certain children or types of children. Such actions may, in effect, expand the legally-protected interests of prospective adopters beyond the scope of such interests in the past.

These policy directions raise important questions about the extent to which adults have an interest that translates into a "right" to adopt or to adopt children of particular characteristics based on personal preference or an assessment of the children who are most likely to be readily available for adoption. Has such a right now been accorded recognition? And, if so, do all adults have the same "right"? Research indicates that, as was the case in early adoption practice [Gill in press], "child welfare practice in adoption is still not particularly inclusive of families of color" [Courtney 1997], and broad organizational and institutional practices may continue to prevent or actively discourage African American and other families of color from adopting [Gilles & Kroll 1991]. Does the law rectify this situation? Does MEPA, for example, require a change in such practices, so that African Americans now have the full opportunity to adopt and, more precisely, to adopt Caucasian infants? Few would contend that African American prospective adoptive parents will benefit significantly from this change in federal law [personal communication with Professor Ruth-Arlene Howe, January 27, 2000].

The issue of "rights" is also tied to market forces related to power, money, and access that may provide greater opportunities for some prospective adoptive parents to realize—to the extent it may exist—the "right" to adopt children of their choosing. The issue of market forces, discussed in greater detail in a previous volume [Freundlich, 2000b], raises important issues related to the extent to which the race and culture of prospective adoptive parents impacts their adoption opportunities.

Informed Decision-Making by Adopters

The second issue bearing on the interests of adults who seek to adopt is the extent to which adoptive parents are given the opportunity to make a fully informed decision about adopting a particular child. In their study, Sorosky, Baran, and Pannor [1984] found that adoptive parents were often denied information about the child they adopted, including the child's background and the actual circumstances leading to the adoption. Agencies, they learned, withheld information from adoptive parents based on "[a]ssumptions about the adoptive parents [that] were often based on biases, faulty theories, lack of trust, and measurement of their strengths and weaknesses that, in fact, did not prove to be true"[1984, p. 85]. More than a decade later, Berry, Barth and Needell [1996] found in their study of more than 1,000 adoptions that over half of the adoptive parents had received no information about the child they were considering for adoption, including any birth, family, or medical history.

Although standards of practice direct that health and other background information about a child and the child's birth family be shared with a prospective adoptive family prior to adoption [Child Welfare League of America 2000],"wrongful adoption" lawsuits have demonstrated that such practice is not uniform. In a number of cases, adoptive parents have demonstrated that adoption agencies failed to provide them with significant information known to the agency about a child's physical, emotional, or developmental problems or with critical background information about the child's birth family and history [Freundlich & Peterson 1998]. Asserting that they would not have adopted the particular child had this information been disclosed, adoptive parents have argued they were deprived of an opportunity to make a fully informed decision and, as a consequence, were not financially or emotionally prepared to respond to their child's significant medical and psychological needs [Freundlich & Peterson 1998]. Courts have recognized the interests of adoptive parents in informed decision-making and held that adoption agencies, as well as independent adoption practitioners, have a duty to disclose known material information about a child's health and social background to prospective adoptive families.

The scope of the interests of prospective adoptive parents in relation to the background of a child whom they are considering for adoption, however, has been subject to debate. Although the wrongful adoption cases make clear that all material health and other background information that is known to an adoption agency or independent practitioner must be disclosed, there is less clarity regarding the extent to which additional information should be gathered and disclosed. There are many issues bearing on disclosure of non-identifying information [Freundlich & Peterson 1998], including:

- To what extent do the interests of prospective adopters require that an agency actively investigate the health and social background of a child and his birth family in order to add to and complete the information given by the birth parents? To what extent would such investigative activities intrude upon the privacy interests of birth parents?

- To what extent should practitioners disclose to prospective adopters unverified suspicions about the background of a child and her birth family, such as the belief, without history or medical indications to support it, that the birth mother consumed alcohol during pregnancy and the child is affected by alcohol exposure? To what extent do such "guesses" inappropriately label children and diminish their opportunities for adoption and expectations for their future?

- To what extent do the interests of prospective adopters support broad genetic testing of children to reassure adopters that children do not have a genetic predisposition for serious diseases in the future? To what extent is such presymptomatic testing contrary to the interests of children?

As these questions illustrate, important interests of adoptive parents may be affected by the interests of others served through adoption. In addition, these issues raise questions as to the extent to which adoptive parents can or should be assured of a child's current and future health and well-being. As litigation has placed greater emphasis on disclosure of background information to adoptive parents, is there an assumption that adoptive parents are entitled not only to background information, but to some level of guarantee regarding the health of a child? An element of the wrongful adoption cases is that adoptive parents would not have adopted the child had they known of the child's or the birth family's history. Does this position reflect an expectation that adoption will provide the family with a "perfect" child—or, at least, that the agency will provide the family with the requisite information to ensure that they minimize the chances of adopting a "defective" one? And how do such expectations fit within the broader realities of parenting? Is any form of parenting risk-free? Or does adoption present special risks against which adoptive parents have certain rights to be protected? If so, how far should those protections go?

The Impact of Adoption on Adoptive Families

A final issue related to the impact of adoption on members of the triad concerns the interests of the adoptive family as a unit comprised of adoptive parents, adopted child, and in some cases, other biological and/or adopted children. The impact of adoption on the adoptive family has not been well addressed in the literature, as little research has been done on adoptive families and little has been written about the adoptive family itself [Cohen et al. 1993]. As a consequence, it is difficult to identify those factors that support or undermine healthy and independent adoptive family functioning. The limited body of research suggests that adoptive families, at least those who adopt children with special needs, tend to be cohesive [Nelson 1985], flexible in roles [Cohen 1984], and less likely than biological families to be seriously disturbed [Tienari et al. 1990]. Similarly, data on the outcomes for adoptive families of healthy infants indicate that the vast majority of these adoptions succeed in the sense that there is a very low disruption rate [Stolley 1993].

The processes of family life for adoptive families, despite their structural differences from biological families, in many ways mirror those in biological families. As Kirk [1984, p. 85] notes, families—whether biological or adoptive—strive for "harmonious relations yielding personal satisfactions; dynamic stability of the family as a group; and the group's permanence." Adoptive families, however, may more strongly seek stability and permanence because, unlike biological parents, adoptive parents do not have the socially and culturally sanctioned status of parenthood as a result of giving birth, and as a result, may feel greater uncertainty about themselves as parents and their family status [Kirk 1984]. Mann's clinical observations of adoptive families [1998] seem to suggest greater stresses associated with achieving stability and permanence. She indicates that adoptive parents often express a sense of responsibility compounded by the understanding that they have chosen to parent another's child; protectiveness of their child; perfectionism; and concerns about their parenting role as a result of "considerable confusion in relation to their unique story within the adoption experience" [1998, p. 49].

There are widely varying perspectives on the nature of adoptive families. At one end of the spectrum, as Hollinger [1996, p. 373] notes, are those who believe adoption creates in all respects a new family that replaces the child's birth family. These advocates, perhaps best represented by the National Council for Adoption, believe that adoptive families function most autonomously when they are structured and regarded "as if" they were biological families [Hollinger 1996, p. 347]. In this construct, family autonomy rests on a notion of exclusivity in parenthood "to allay [adoptive parents'] insecurities about their own parenting abilities and the permanence of adoption" [Appell 1996, p. 490]. By contrast, there are those that believe that nonexclusivity is consistent with adoptive family autonomy and, further, promotes the adoptive family's sense of entitlement to the child [Groth 1987; Bradbury & Marsh 1988]. Kirk [1984], for example, notes that when adoptive parents are able to recognize the role of their child's birth parents, dynamic family stability is promoted and family satisfaction is advanced.

Autonomy of the adoptive family is perhaps most clear from a legal perspective. Legally, the adoptive family is equivalent to the birth family. The law attempts to promote the integrity of the adoptive family by providing it with the authority to determine what is best for the family and the adopted child without state interference and by promoting the interests of children in having secure legal and emotional ties to the people who parent them [Hollinger 1998]. The autonomy and integrity of the adoptive family, however, appear more complicated than this legal framework would appear to suggest, both in terms of social perceptions of its "realness" or authenticity as a family and issues related to the integrity of the adoptive family in light of greater openness in adoption.

The Authenticity of the Adoptive Family

Issues related to the "realness" or authenticity of the family that is formed through adoption arise in the context of societal views of adoptive families. These views tend to be complex, with positive, if not romanticized, concepts of adoptive families on the one hand, and negative stereotypes that stigmatize adoptive parents and consequently diminish adoptive families on the other. Mann [1998, p. 46] contends that views of adoptive families flow from simplistic views of adoptive parents—they are either "wonderful Christian people" or they are people who "take someone's child." Both characterizations have significant implications regarding the authenticity of the adoptive family.

At one end of the sociocultural spectrum of attitudes is the view of adoptive parents as altruistic, nobly rescuing a child from abandonment or horrific conditions. Adoptive parents in this view undertake a charitable endeavor in adopting, and although ostensibly positive in its appreciation of adoptive parents, it tends to diminish adoptive parents by assuming that kindness rather than the desire to have a genuine parent-child relationship motivates them. The authenticity of the adoptive family is likely to be put into doubt if the basis of family formation is assumed to be humanitarianism and the nature of the parent-child relationship to be that of rescuer and rescued.

The other end of the spectrum of attitudes regarding adoptive parents—described by Mann [1998] as the view that adoptive parents have "taken" the children of others—may be more pervasive and as a result, have greater impact on the perceived "realness" of adoptive families. In a social and cultural environment that largely defines kinship in terms of biological relationships [Kirk 1984], the genuineness of adoptive families may be put into doubt. Some express concerns that the biological nature of kinship has been taken to the level of biological essentialism [Hollinger 1998]—that is, a belief in the essential validity of biological connections alone—leaving little as a genuine basis for the relationship between adoptive parents and children. Adoption, instead, may be relegated to the status of a "cultural fiction" [Miall 1987]. The construct of a "primal wound" associated with a child's placement for adoption [Verrier 1993]—a wound that cannot be healed by adoptive parents—may reinforce the concept that the "real" family—the only family meaningful for the child—exists on the basis of a biological bond.

Biological essentialism, however, as an absolutist perspective, may not accurately reflect prevailing social and cultural views of "family" in general and adoptive families in particular. Rather than an outright rejection of adoptive families as inauthentic, there instead may be more subtle forces at work that stigmatize adoptive families at some level as "less than real." In his work, *Shared Fate* [1984], Kirk described the types of attitudes that adoptive parents frequently encountered from others, experiences that indicated that others made a sharp distinction between adoptive and biological parenthood, often relegating adoptive parenthood and family to "substitutive" and "second best" status. Adoptive parents, for example, reported that they frequently encountered remarks from others such as, "This child looks so much like you—he(she) could be your own" and "Isn't it wonderful of you to have taken this child" [Kirk 1984, p. 30]. The literature of the late 1980s and early 1990s further elaborated on this stigmatization of adoptive parents and adoptive families [Hoffman-Riem 1989; Miall 1987; Kaye 1990].

There are different views of the impact of the biological parenthood-adoptive parenthood dichotomy. Some believe that the differences between biological and adoptive families can enhance the strengths of both types of families. Hoffman-Riem [1989, p. 28] describes the adoptive family as "a social type of family with dual parenthood"—social parenthood and biological parenthood. She believes that this "structural peculiarity" gives rise to the conflicts regarding the nature of "real, authentic parenthood" and the authenticity of adoptive families, but she contends that acknowledgment of social parenthood as the basis of the adoptive family is what imbues the adoptive family with authenticity [1989, p. 28]. Kirk, in his seminal work *Shared Fate* [1984], emphasized the value of adoptive parents' "acknowledgment of differences" between birth parenting and adoptive parenting. He found that considerable strengths accompanied the capacity of adoptive parents to acknowledge these differences, finding higher levels of empathy, communication, and parental satisfaction with adoption in these families. Benefits to adoptive families as well as to society may flow from acknowledgment of the dual parenthood that characterizes adoptive families. Hoffman-Reim [1989, p. 26] writes:

> Because biological parents take the normality of their families for granted, some basic ideas about what constitutes a family remain implicit. The way adoptive parents think about having a child, or about the quality of their relationships with the child, uncovers some basic conceptions of kinship, parenthood, and authentic family life for all of us.

Mann [1998] is far less optimistic about the benefits of the acknowledgment of differences approach for adoptive families. She maintains that by comparing themselves to "normal" birth families, adoptive families position themselves as "second rate." She contends that these comparisons lay at the heart of the question of what is "real authentic parenting" and that stigmatization has eroded the ability of adoptive families to fully embrace the concept of their own authenticity [1998, p. 45].

The extent to which adoptive families are socially stigmatized has been examined by few surveys. Miall [1987], for example, found that adoptive parents were aware of public attitudes and beliefs about adoption that suggested that the public viewed adoptive families as "lesser" families: beliefs that love and bonding in adoption were "second best" to birth family relationships and views that adoptive families were not "real" families. Similarly, a more recent public opinion survey focused on Americans' attitudes about adoption found that almost one-half of the respondents believed that adoption, while preferable to remaining childless, was not "as good as" having a biological child of one's own [Evan B. Donaldson Adoption Institute 1997]. A significant percentage of those surveyed questioned whether the love between adoptive parents and their children could be as strong as the love between birth parents and their children [Evan B. Donaldson Adoption Institute 1997].

The media may reinforce views of adoptive parents and adoptive families as less than authentic in the same ways that negative portrayals of adoptees and birth parents have raised questions in the public's mind about the integrity and stability of these triad members. On the one hand, the media has focused on baby-buying involving affluent prospective adoptive parents and shady intermediaries, stories that may suggest that adoptive parents essentially purchase parenthood status as they would any other commodity. In the same vein, media coverage has highlighted decisions of adoptive parents to "return" difficult-to-manage children adopted from other countries, implicitly or explicitly suggesting that parents are seeking "designer" children and will readily discard "inferior" products. Such stories, irrespective of the extent to which they accurately present the majority of adoptions, may suggest to the public that adoptive family life is based on factors other than the authentic bonds that characterize biologically constituted families.

The other thrust of media coverage—highlighting happy reunions of adult adoptees with their birth parents—may convey an equally powerful message about the nature of adoptive families. These stories, which frequently refer to birth parents as the "real parents" and fail to even mention the adoptive parents, may suggest that adoptive families are merely way-stations for children until they mature and reconnect with their "real" families. Such stories, like those that convey more negative messages about adoptive parenting, may play to stereotypes of the adoptive family as substitutive and second-best.

It may be that the media reflects existing societal views and uncertainties about adoptive families. Increasing diversity in U.S. families—through divorce and remarriage, reproductive technology, and nontraditional parenting relationships—may ultimately bring perceptions of adoptive families as "substitutive" or "second best" to an end. In the meantime, there appears to be a remarkable persistence in societal attitudes about the genuineness of adoptive families, an issue that may become more complex as openness in adoption becomes more pervasive.

The Adoptive Family and Issues of Openness

A consideration of the impact of adoption on the adoptive family unit, by necessity, must take into account the growing practice of openness in adoption. Openness—in all of its many forms—has come to be considered an appropriate, if not the most appropriate, form of adoption [Appell 1996]. With this development, questions have been raised as to whether the nature and integrity of the adoptive family inherently change when an adoption is "open." As discussed earlier, the aspect of openness most broadly practiced is birth parent selection of the adoptive parent for her child—a practice that raises a number of questions related to the impact on adoptive families. Do adoptive parents experience "choosing" differently when birth parents, as opposed to social workers, select them to adopt their child? Is one process more or less threatening than the other to adoptive parents—particularly given an environment in which the "competition" for a child is perceived as increasingly intense [see Rosenberg 1992, p. 169]? Does "too much choice" in the adoption process, as Modell [1994] writes, conflict with prevailing notions of parenthood that weave into parenting a sense of destiny and inevitability? On the other hand, does placing greater power to choose in the hands of birth parents—with the choice based perhaps more on an intuitive sense of adoptive parent "rightness" than on the social workers' alleged "objective" factors—make adoption seem more "like" biological parenthood?

Openness is commonly viewed as involving not only birth parent selection of adoptive parents, but ongoing communication between birth and adoptive families at some level. Birth parents and adoptive parents, at minimum, meet and exchange identifying information [Baran & Pannor 1990], and in the more fully developed forms of openness, develop an ongoing relationship [Gritter 1997]. Because openness in the relationship sense involves "an uncharted and certainly challenging way of surrendering and taking on parenthood" [Modell 1994, p. 56], many questions remain unresolved, particularly in relation to its impact on adoptive parents:

> Does the current emphasis on openness, in effect, coerce adoptive parents who feel they must be willing to maintain contact with birth parents or lose the opportunity to adopt [Mann 1998]?

> Does openness intrude on the adoptive family's ability to function as a family, creating an environment in which, as Hoffman-Riem [1989, p. 28] writes, "the birth parents may penetrate deep into the reality of adoptive family life"?

> Do enforceable agreements for contact between adoptive and birth families after the adoption is finalized undermine the well-being of the adoptive family by creating the

possibility of ongoing court involvement in their lives [Hollinger 1996]?

Perceptions of the impact of openness on adoptive family well-being vary. On the one hand, concerns are expressed that birth parents' expectations of openness at the time of adoptive placements may place pressure on adoptive parents to accede to ongoing relationships out of a fear that resistance would cause them to lose the opportunity to adopt [Mann 1998]. There likewise is the concern that openness may demand that adoptive parents accept the fact that their children will have "two sets of parents" and may force them to agree to co-parenting with birth parents [Mann 1998, p. 44]. Modell [1994, p. 232] notes that objections to openness in adoption may also be based on fears that a relationship based on "paper" cannot successfully compete against the presence of "blood ties" and a belief, as stated by Smith and Miroff [1987, pp. 7, 118], that the "process of parental entitlement can only occur through the unconditional severance of earlier parental ties."

Those who express concerns about the impact of openness on the adoptive family find the potential incursions into the adoptive family at odds with the clearly defined legal status of adoptive parents that gives them the same legal rights and responsibilities as other parents, including the authority to rear their child "in accord with their own parental prerogatives" [Hollinger 1996, p. 373]. Hollinger [1996, p. 373] notes that these prerogatives of adoptive families include the adoptive parents' freedom to decide who may or may not visit or communicate with the child, and thus, finds the ongoing involvement of birth parents inherently problematic. She notes a "shift in power from adoptive to birth parents" in which, given the current "seller's market," birth parents have the ability to "insist on becoming and remaining a part of the new adoptive family's life." She describes this process as one in which adoption professionals have become "willing agents" in supporting the exercise of power by birth parents over adoptive parents. Modell notes that the concept of openness in adoption "strikes a chill—especially in adoptive parents, but in the general public as well" [1994, pp. 230-231]. She notes that:

Open adoption is not greeted with the fascination and appreciation that a reunion between long-lost kin is, even when those kin were not supposed to know one another. Reunions are perceived as reactivating existing, natural bonds, whereas open adoptions are seen as permitting people to construct "unnatural" bonds, on purpose and from the very beginning. Above all, open adoption is disturbing because it does not allow adoptive kinship to be just like biological kinship [1994, p. 231].

Of particular concern to those who see negative effects from openness on the well-being of the adoptive family are enforceable postadoption contact agreements [Hollinger 1996]. At one level is the extent to which such agreements may jeopardize the validity of the adoption. The validity of an adoption, however, has been clearly separated from issues related to adherence to postadoption contact agreements in the laws of those states that have endorsed the enforceability of postadoption contact agreements of any sort [Evan B. Donaldson Adoption Institute 1999a]. In line with the approach recommended by the Uniform Adoption Act [§ 3-707], these laws provide that the validity of an adoption cannot be challenged because a party has failed to comply with a postadoption visitation agreement [Appell 1996]. These state laws attempt to balance the interests of adoptive families—by providing a structure for ensuring the integrity of adoptions in which openness has been contractually agreed upon—with the interests of the members of the triad in sustaining an ongoing relationship.

The issue that continues to be debated is the extent to which adoptive parents see open adoption as an intrusion into the integrity of their family. Do adoptive parents experience open arrangements with birth parents as intrusive co-parenting, as many critics of openness consistently posit as a harmful outcome of openness? Little research has addressed this issue. In one of the few studies on adoptive parents' views of the impact of openness on their families, Siegel [1993] probed the sentiments of 21 adoptive couples in open adoption arrangements. She found that despite initial fears and concerns about openness, most of the respondents identified advantages of open adoption that appeared to be associated with autonomous parenting and family functioning. They reported that open adoption gave them a sense of control with regard to birth parents; prepared them to effectively fulfill their roles as parents; dissolved fantasies about their child's birth parents; and alleviated guilt and any moral apprehension about "having someone else's child" [1993, p. 18]. Interestingly, the adoptive parents reported that openness was "simply not that much of a concern" when weighed against the more difficult issues of infertility; finding a child to adopt; "dealing with unresponsive and obstructive social workers, lawyers, and medical personnel;" and coping with the lifelong issues involved in every adoption [1993, p. 20].

Other research on the impact of open adoption on adoptive families likewise indicates that the "concerns and dire warnings of open adoption critics" have not come to fruition [Brodzinsky et al. 1998, p. 83]. Studies have found that adoptive parents in open arrangements report positive benefits for themselves and their families, including a high level of satisfaction with openness and good relationships with birth parents [Belbas 1987; Etter 1993; Gross 1993]; a greater sense of entitlement to their child [McRoy & Grotevant 1988a; Belbas 1987]; fewer concerns about attachment issues [Silverstein & Demick 1994]; and less concern about efforts by birth parents to reclaim their child [Belbas 1987]. Modell notes that openness can validate the strength of the relationship created through adoption by establishing a parallel, rather than substitutive, kinship relationship. She writes:

> Open adoption introduces not "alternative parenthood" but alternative parents, and the distinction is not trivial. One parent is not "real," the other "unreal"; one is not "natural" and the other "fictive" [1994, p. 232].

The concerns expressed by those fearful of the encroachment posed by open adoption on the well-being of the adoptive family do not appear to be borne out by the research at this juncture. Instead, the research suggests that adoptive parents in general do not see birth parents as "penetrating" adoptive family life in unwholesome ways. At the same time, as Modell points out, "neither [the adoptive nor birth] parent has a script for such sharing or a map for this kinship" [1994, p. 56]. She [1994, p. 56] observes:

> An adoptive parent shares with rather than substitutes for a birth parent; a birth parent is kin but not parent to the child. Because this is confusing, the arrangement demands creativity about the roles of being related and the meanings of "mother," "father," and "kin."

The complexity of these issues has suggested to some that "surrounding the adoption circle" with postadoption services—for birth parents, adoptive parents, and adoptees—is critical. On the issue of postadoption support, Rosenberg [1992, pp. 184-185] states that:

> [T]he acknowledgment of participants' special developmental tasks should include normalizing the possible need for post adoption services....Birth parents or adoptive parents may find that the original contract [agreeing to openness] is unworkable in some way, particularly with children's changing developmental needs. One or both parties may request a shift in the contract toward more or less contact. Such requests for shifts must be dealt with respectfully and must be considered part of the development of the adoptive family circle.

These considerations highlight the importance of ongoing support of families as their kinship relationships continue to develop and evolve. They also emphasize the importance of developing a better understanding of the impact of openness on the adopted person as he or she develops, an issue that is only beginning to be studied [Grotevant & McRoy 1998].

Summary

The psychological and social processes that characterize the transition to the status of adoptive parent highlight the vulnerabilities associated with infertility in an environment that bases the concept of parenthood on biological ties. Achieving a sense of identity as "parent" may present particular challenges for individuals who desire to but cannot achieve biological parenthood. A sense of true "parenthood," however, may be difficult to achieve even by those who adopt for reasons other than infertility because of prevailing notions that biology dictates "real" parent status. The vulnerabilities of prospective adoptive parents emphasize the potential impact of the administrative and legal processes leading to approval or rejection of individuals as adoptive parents. The traditional assessment process—criticized because of its vaguely defined criteria and susceptibility to subjective determinations and varying outcomes—raises questions related to inherent validity and fairness to prospective adoptive parents. How should prospective adoptive parents be evaluated? What criteria indicate that an individual would be a "good" adoptive parent?

The issues related to validity and fairness of the assessment process from the perspective of prospective adoptive parents, however, also must be viewed in the context of growing concerns that the rights of adults in relation to adoption have become overarching. Have adult interests in adopting translated into a "right" to adopt? Do adults not only have the right to consider only certain types of children for adoption but to insist that a specified type of child be placed with them (such as a biracial infant if a Caucasian infant is not available)? Although child welfare professionals and organizations continue to stress that adoption is a service for children [Child Welfare League of America 2000], there are increasing legal protections for adults who claim to have been subject to unfair discrimination when a child is not placed with them. To what extent do adults' interests in adopting translate into rights? What weight should be accorded adults' interests in adopting—and specifically their adoption preferences?

There also are important issues related to informed decision-making by prospective adoptive parents with regard to the adoption of a child. What is the appropriate scope of the duty of adoption professionals to provide prospective adoptive parents with background information on a child they are considering for adoption? Are there countervailing interests that may limit the scope of such disclosures?

The impact of adoption on the adoptive family as a unit may be characterized by both external and internal forces, all of which bear on the authenticity or "realness" of the adoptive family. Adoptive families may be characterized as heroic, rescuing children in need; suspect for having taken "someone else's child"; or "second best" as they resort to adoption, having failed to reproduce biologically. The differences between biological and adoptive parenting have been interpreted as both strengths and vulnerabilities, promoting the family's sense of well-being, according to some, and detracting from their sense of wholeness, according to others. Media coverage of adoption may highlight these tensions by focusing, on the one hand, on the "acquisition" of children by adoptive parents through dubious means and, on the other hand, on the reunions of adoptees and their birth families as reflective of the connections of "real" family.

Much remains to be understood about openness in adoption. It is clear that open adoptions are occurring in greater numbers and in a variety of forms: some adoptive parents resist but reluctantly agree to ongoing contact with birth families; other adoptive parents and birth parents enter into mutually desired relationships with one another that vary, according to the joint wishes of the adults, in the nature and degree of contact; and in yet other situations, adoptive parents express greater interest in ongoing connections with birth parents than do the birth parents themselves. Research and clinical experience suggest that openness does not undermine the authenticity of the adoptive family, but some remain skeptical. As openness continues to erode the traditional notions of exclusivity and secrecy in adoption, much will be learned about the impact of openness on adoptive families and the extent to which a new adoption paradigm serves the interests of all members of the triad.

Conclusion

In any consideration of ethical issues in adoption, there is no more important area of focus than the impact of adoption on members of the triad. If policy and practice are to be responsive to the needs and interests of adopted individuals (both children and adults), birth mothers and birth fathers, prospective adoptive parents, and adoptive families, an understanding of the effects of past and current policy and practice is critical. The complexities surrounding adoption—both in terms of the range of issues that impact triad members and the potential for tensions among the respective rights, interests and needs of triad members—has made such an understanding difficult to reach. Nonetheless, this volume has attempted to outline the key issues that affect each member of the triad, the conflicting perspectives on the experiences of triad members, and the key challenges in shaping future policy and practice in ethical ways.

Gritter [1997, p. 36] identifies the "overarching value of respect" for all members of the triad as crucial to quality adoption policy and practice. He [1997] writes that from the value of respect, eight closely related values flow, values that can help to shape future policy and practice. These values are honor for the adoptee whose needs are paramount; candor with all triad members about all aspects of adoption; responsibility for decisions that are freely chosen; recognition of the pain that is integral to adoption; integrity in holding true to the commitments made in adoption; adaptability in the face of dynamic adoptive relationships; acknowledgment of the life-altering nature of adoption; and community, the recognition that each participant in adoption affects and is affected by the other participants [Gritter 1997].

Similarly, Pavao [1998, p. xi] writes that adoption should be viewed as "a whole system, [in which] everyone involved [feels] some empathy for the other members of the adoption world and...thereby grow[s] and heal[s] themselves." Her conclusion [1998, p. xv] about the benefits of ethical adoption policy and practice provides the touchstone for shaping the adoption in the future:

> When adoption is done ethically, when it is the right thing for all of the parents, birth and adoptive, when the extended families have been educated and worked with and when the community is well prepared, then we all know we have expanded our lives, expanded our families, and expanded our hearts.

References

Abbey, A., Andrews, F. M., & Halman, L. J. (1992). Infertility and subjective well-being: The mediating roles of self-esteem, internal control, and interpersonal conflict. *Journal of Marriage and the Family, 54*, 408–417.

Adams v. Monroe County (1998). 21 F.Supp.2d 235 (W.D.N.Y).

Ae Ran Won. (2000). Annual Report 1999. Seoul, Korea: Author.

AFCARS Report (2000, May 16). *The AFCARS Report*. [On-line]. Available: http://www/acf.dhhs.gov/programs/cb/stats/tareport/rpt0100/ar0100.htm

ALMA v. Mellon. (1979). 601 F. 2d 1225 (2d Cir.).

Altstein, H. & Simon, R. (1991). *Intercountry Adoption: A Multinational Perspective*. New York: Praeger Publishers.

Anthony, E. J. (1990). Foreword. In D. M. Brodzinsky & M. D. Schechter (Eds.), *The psychology of adoption* (pp. vii–viii). New York: Oxford University Press.

Appell, A.R. (1996). The move toward legally sanctioned cooperative adoption: Can it survive the Uniform Adoption Act? *Family Law Quarterly, 30*(2), 483–518.

Appell, A. R. & Boyer, B. A. (1995). Parental rights vs. best interests of the child: A false dichotomy in the context of adoption. *Duke Journal of Gender Law & Policy, 2*(1), 63–83.

Arndt, M. (1986). Severed roots: The sealed adoption records controversy. *Northern Illinois University Law Review, 6*, 103–27.

Aronson, J. E. (2000). Alcohol related disorders and children adopted from abroad. In R. P. Barth, M. Freundlich & D. Brodzinsky (Eds.), *Adoption and prenatal alcohol and drug exposure: Research, policy and practice* (pp. 147–169). Washington, DC: CWLA Press.

Aumend, S. & Barrett, M. (1984). Self-concept and attitudes toward adoption: A comparison of searching and non-searching adult adoptees. *Child Welfare, 63*, 251–259.

Auth, P. J. & Zaret, S. (1986). The search in adoption: A service and a process. *Social Casework, 67*, 560–68.

171

Avery, R. J. (1998). Information disclosure and openness in adoption: State policy and empirical evidence. *Children & Youth Services Review, 20*, 57–75.

Axness, M. W. (1994 July/August/September). Painful lessons. *Roots and Wings*, 5–7.

Axness, M. W. (1999a). A different kind of relationship: Thoughts on adoption—An interview with Nancy Verrier. [On-line]. Available: http://www.birthpsychology.com/birthscene/adoption8.html

Axness, M. W. (1999b). Between adoptive parents and birth mothers: More thoughts on "A different kind of relationship"—Responses to the Nancy Verrier interview on contemporary adoption issues. *Adoption Insight*, 1–5.

Axness, M. W. & Shaw, B. (1999, November 4). *Does adoption respect the interests of birthparents and birth family members?* Presentation at the conference, Ethics and Adoption: Challenges for Today and the Future, Anaheim, CA (Presented by the Evan B. Donaldson Adoption Institute).

Babb, L. A. (1995). *A study of ethics in contemporary adoption practice in the United States.* Unpublished Ph.D. dissertation, California Coast University, Santa Ana, California.

Bachrach, C. A. (1986). Adoption plans, adopted children, and adoptive mothers. *Journal of Marriage and the Family, 48,* 243–253.

Bachrach, C. A., Adams, P. F., Sambrano, S., & London, K. A. (1990). Adoption in the 1980s. *Advance Data from Vital and Health Statistics, No. 181.* Hyattsville, MD: National Center for Health Statistics.

Bachrach, C. A., Stolley, K. S., & London, K. A. (1992). Relinquishment of premarital births: Evidence from national survey data. *Family Planning Perspectives, 24*(1), 27–32.

Baldwin, W. H. (1976). Adolescent pregnancy and childbearing: Growing concerns for Americans. *Population Bulletin, 31*(2), 2–34.

Banks, R. R. (1998). The color of desire: Fulfilling adoptive parents' racial preferences through discriminatory state action. *The Yale Law Journal, 107,* 875–964.

Baran, A. & Pannor, R. (1990). Open adoption. In D. M. Brodzinsky & M. D. Schechter (Eds.), *Psychology of adoption* (pp. 316–331). New York: Oxford University Press.

Baran, A., Pannor, R., & Sorosky, A.D. (1976). Open adoption. *Social Work, 21,* 97–100.

Baran, A., Pannor, R., & Sorosky, A.D. (1977). The lingering pain of surrendering a child. *Psychology Today, 11*(1), 58–60.

Barker, S., Byrne, S., Morrison, M., & Spenser, M. (1998). *Preparing for permanence. Assessment: Points to consider for those assessing potential adopters and foster carers.* London: British Agencies for Adoption and Fostering.

Barth, R. P. & Berry, M. (1988). *Adoption and disruption: Rates, risks, and responses.* New York: Aldine De Gruyter.

Bartholet, E. (1993a). *Family bonds: Adoption and the politics of parenting.* Boston: Houghton Mifflin Company.

Bartholet, E. (1993b, July 13). Op-Ed: Blood parents vs. real parents. *The New York Times,* p. A19.

Bartholet, E. (1993c). International adoption: Current status and future prospects. *The Future of Adoption, 3*(1), 89–103.

Bartholet, E. (1996). International adoption: Propriety, prospects, and pragmatics. *Journal of American Academy of Matrimonial Lawyers, 13*(2), 181–210.

Bartholet, E. (1998). Private race preferences in family formation. *Yale Law Journal, 107*(7), 2351– 2356.

Belbas, N. (1987). Staying in touch: Empathy in open adoptions. *Smith College Studies in Social Work, 57,* 184–198.

Belkin, L. (1998, April 5). Now accepting applications for my baby. *The New York Times Magazine,* 58–62.

Bell, W. (1965). *Aid to dependent children.* New York: Columbia University Press.

Benson, P., Sharma, A. & Roehlkepartain, E. C. (1994). *Growing up adopted.* Minneapolis: Search Institute.

Berry, M. (1991). The effects of open adoption on biological and adoptive parents and the children: The arguments and the evidence. *Child Welfare, 70,* 637–651.

Berry, M., Barth, R. P., & Needell, B. (1996). Preparation, support and satisfaction of adoptive families in agency and independent adoptions. *Child and Adolescent Social Work Journal, 13*(2), 157–183.

Blum, L. H. (1976). When adoptive families ask for help. *Primary Care, 3*, 241–249.

Blum, R. W., Resnick, M. D., & Stark, T. (1987). The impact of a parental notification law on adolescent abortion decision-making. *American Journal of Public Health, 77*, 619–620.

Bohman, M. (1970) *Adopted children and their families: A follow-up study of adopted children, their background environment, and adjustment.* Stockholm, Sweden: Proprius.

Bohman, M. & Sigvardsson, S. (1990). Outcome in adoption: Lessons from longitudinal studies. In D. M. Brodzinsky & M. D. Schechter (Eds.), *The psychology of adoption* (pp. 93–106). New York: Oxford University Press.

Bohman, M. & Von Knorring, A. L. (1979). Psychiatric illness among adults adopted as infants. *Acia Paediatrica Scandinavica, 60*, 106–112.

Bonnet, C. (1993). Adoption at birth: Prevention against abandonment or neonaticide. *Child Abuse and Neglect, 17*(4), 501–513.

Borgman, R. (1981). Antecedents and consequences of parental rights termination for abused and neglected children. *Child Welfare, 60*, 391–404.

Boss, P. (1992). *Adoption in Australia: A comparative study of Australian adoption and legislation and policy.* Notting Hill, Victoria: National Children's Bureau of Australia.

Bouchier, P., Lambert, L., & Triseliotis, J. (1991). *Parting with a child for adoption: The mother's perspective.* London: British Association of Adoption and Fostering.

Bradbury S. & Marsh, M. (1988). Linking families in preadoption counseling: A family systems model. *Child Welfare, 67*, 327–334.

Brazelton, T. B. (1989). *Families: Crises and caring.* Reading, MA: Addison-Wesley.

Brodzinsky, A. B. (1990). Surrendering an infant for adoption: The birth mother experience. In D. M. Brodzinsky & M.D. Schechter (Eds.), *The psychology of adoption* (pp. 295–315). New York: Oxford University Press.

Brodzinksy, D. M. (1987). Adjustment to adoption: A psychosocial perspective. *Clinical Psychology Review, 7*, 25–47.

Brodzinsky, D. M. (1990). A stress and coping model of adoption adjustment. In D. M. Brodzinsky & M. D. Schechter (Eds.), *The psychology of adoption* (pp. 3–24). New York: Oxford University Press.

Brodzinsky, D. M. (1993). Long term outcomes in adoption. *The Future of Children, 3*(1), 153–166.

Brodzinsky, D. M., Lang, R., & Smith, D. (1995). Parenting adopted children. In M. H. Bornstein (Ed.), *Handbook of parenting: Vol. 3. Status and social conditions of parenting* (pp. 209–232). Mahwah, NJ: Erlbaum.

Brodzinsky, D. M., Schechter, M. D., Braff, A. M., & Singer, L. M. (1984). Psychological and academic adjustment in adoption children. *Journal of Consulting and Clinical Psychology, 52*, 582–590.

Brodzinsky, D. M., Schechter, M. D., & Brodzinsky, A. B. (1986). Children's knowledge of adoption: Developmental changes and implications for adjustment. In R. Ashmore & D. M. Brodzinsky (Eds.), *Thinking about the family: Views of parents and children* (pp. 205–232). Hillsdale, NY: Erlbaum.

Brodzinsky, D., Smith, D. W., & Brodzinsky, A. B. (1998). *Children's adjustment to adoption: Developmental and clinical issues.* Thousands Oaks, CA: Sage Publications.

Brown, E. G. & Brieland, D. (1975). Adoptive screening: New data, new dilemmas. *Social Work, 20*(4), 291–295.

Burns, L. H. (1987). Infertility as boundary ambiguity: One theoretical perspective. *Family Process, 26*, 359–372.

Butler, R. R. & Koralski, S. (1990). Infertility: A crisis with no resolution. *Journal of Mental Health Counseling, 12*, 151–163.

Byrd, A. D. (1988). The case for confidential adoptions. *Public Welfare, 46*(4), 20–23.

Byrd, D. (1999). Open adoption: Who benefits? In C. Marshner & W. L. Pierce (Eds.), *Adoption Factbook III* (pp. 413–416). Washington, D.C.: National Council for Adoption.

Caban v. Mohammed. (1979). 441 U.S. 380.

Cadoret, R. J. (1990). Biologic perspectives of adoptee adjustment. In D. M. Brodzinsky & M. D. Schechter (Eds.), *The psychology of adoption* (pp. 25–41). New York: Oxford University Press.

Cahn, N. & Singer, J. (In press). Adoption, identity and the Constitution: The case for opening closed records. *University of Pennsylvania Journal of Constitutional Law.*

Campbell, L. H., Silverman, P. R., & Patti, P. B. (1991). Reunions between adoptees and birth parents: The adoptees' experience. *Social Work, 36*, 329–335.

Card, J. J. & Wise, L. L. (1981). Teenage mothers and teenage fathers: The impact of early childbearing on the parents' personal and professional lives. In F. F. Furstenberg, Jr., R. Lincoln, & J. Menken (Eds.), *Teenage sexuality, pregnancy and childbearing* (pp. 211–222). Philadelphia: University of Pennsylvania.

Carey, W. B., Lipton, W. L., & Myers, R. A. (1974). Temperament in adopted and foster babies. *Child Welfare, 53*, 352–359.

Carp, E. W. (1998). *Family matters: Secrecy and disclosure in the history of adoption*. Cambridge, MA: Harvard University Press.

Chandra, A., Abma, J., Maza, P., & Bachrach, C. (1999, May 11). Adoption, adoption seeking, and relinquishment for adoption in the United States. *Advance Data, 306*. Washington, DC: U.S. Department of Health and Human Services, Centers for Disease Control, National Center for Health Statistics.

Chapin Hall Center for Children. (1997). *An update from the multistate foster care data archive: Foster care dynamics 1983–1994*. Chicago: Chapin Hall Center for Children at the University of Chicago.

Charlton, L., Crank, M., Kansara, K., & Oliver, C. (1998). *Still screaming: Birthparents compulsorily separated from their children*. Manchester, England: After Adoption.

Child Welfare League of America. (2000). *Standards for adoption service* (Rev. ed.). Washington, DC: Child Welfare League of America.

Chippindale-Bakker, V. & Foster, L. (1996). Adoption in the 1990s: Sociodemographic determinants of biological parents choosing adoption. *Child Welfare, 75*, 337–355.

Cicchini, M. (1993). *The development of responsibility: The experience of birth fathers in adoption*. Sydney, Australia: Adoption Research and Counseling Services, Inc.

Clapton, G. (1997). Birth fathers, the adoption process and fatherhood. *Adoption & Fostering, 21*(1), 29–36.

Clark, I., McWilliam, E., & Phillips, R. (1998). Empowering prospective adopters. *Adoption & Fostering, 22*(2), 35–43.

Cocozzelli, C. (1989). Predicting the decision of biological mothers to retain or relinquish their babies for adoption: Implications for open placement. *Child Welfare, 68*, 33–44.

Cohen, J. (1984). Adoption breakdown with older children. In P. Sachdev (Ed.), *Adoption: Current issues and trends* (pp. 129–138). Toronto: Butterworths.

Cohen, N. J., Coyne, J., & Duvall, J. (1993). Adopted and biological children in the clinic: Family, parental and child characteristics. *Journal of Child Psychology and Psychiatry, 34*, 545–562.

Cole, E. S. (1985). Adoption: History, policy, and program. In J. Laird and A. Hartman (Eds.), *Handbook of Child Welfare* (pp. 13–26). New York: The Free Press.

Cole, E. S. & Donley, K. S. (1990). History, values, and placement policy issues in adoption. In D. Brodzinsky & M. Schechter (Eds.), *The psychology of adoption* (pp. 273–294). New York/Oxford: Oxford University Press.

Concerned United Birthparents. (2000, January 3). What is CUB? [On-line]. Available: http://www.webnations.com/cub/page9.htm

Condon, J. T. (1986). Psychological disability in women who relinquish a baby for adoption. *Medical Journal of Australia, 144*, 117–119.

Costin, L. (1972). *Child welfare: Policies and practices.* New York: McGraw Hill.

Courtney, M. (1997). The politics and realities of transracial adoption. *Child Welfare, 76*, 749–780.

Coyne, J., Duvall, J., & Cohen, N. J. (1991, November 2). *Special issues in brief therapy with adoptive families.* Paper presented at the 49th Annual Conference of the American Association for Marriage and Family Therapy, Dallas, TX.

Craig, T. L. (1998). Establishing the biological rights doctrine to protect unwed fathers in contested adoptions. *Florida State University Law Review, 25*, 391–438.

Curtis, P. A. (1990). An ethnographic study of pregnancy counseling. *Clinical Social Work Journal, 18*(3), 243–256.

Cushman, L. F., Kalmuss, D., & Namerow, P. B. (1993). Placing an infant for adoption: The experiences of young birth mothers. *Social Work, 38*, 264–272.

Custer, M. (1993). Adoption as an option for unmarried pregnant teens. *Adolescence, 28*(112), 891–902.

Dalby, J. T., Fox, S. & Haslam, R. H. (1982). Adoption and foster care rates in pediatric disorders. *Developmental and Behavioral Pediatrics, 3*, 61–64.

Daly, K. J. (1992). Toward a formal theory of interactive resocialization: The case of adoptive parenthood. *Qualitative Sociology, 15*(4), 395–417.

Daly, K. J. (1988). Reshaped parenthood identity: The transition to adoptive parenthood. *Journal of Contemporary Ethnography, 17,* 40–66.

Daly, K. J. & Sobol, M. P. (1994, January). Public and private adoption: A comparison of service and accessibility. *Family Relations,* 86–93.

Day, C. & Leeding, A. (1980). *Access to birth records: The impact of section 26 of the Children Act 1975.* (Research Series No. 1). London: Association of British Adoption and Fostering Agencies.

Department of the Army Staff Communications Office. Box 19, RG 319. Washington, DC: National Archives.

Deykin, E. Y., Campbell, L., & Patti, P. (1984). The post adoption experience of surrendering parents. *American Journal of Orthopsychiatry, 54,* 271–280.

Deykin, E. Y., Patti, P., & Ryan, J. (1988). Fathers of adopted children: A study on the impact of child surrender on birthfathers. *American Journal of Orthopsychiatry, 58,* 240–248.

Dickson, I. R., Heffron, W. M., & Parker, C. (1990). Children from disrupted and adoptive homes on an inpatient unit. *American Journal of Orthopsychiatry, 60,* 594–602.

Doe v. Sunquist. (1999). No. 01-S-01-9901-CV-00006(Tenn.). [On-line]. Available:http://www.tsc.state.tn.us/OPINIONS/TSC/Sc3qtr99.htm.

Donnelly, B. W. & Voydanoff, P. (1996). Parenting versus placing for adoption: Consequences for adolescent mothers. *Family Relations, 45,* 427–434.

Dorow, S. (Ed.). (1999). *I wish for you a beautiful life: Letters from the Korean birth mothers of Ae Ran Won to their children.* St. Paul, MN: Yeong and Yeong Book Company.

Dreyfuss, R. C. & Nelkin, D. (1992). The jurisprudence of genetics. *Vanderbilt Law Review, 45,* 313–345.

Dukette, R. (1984). Values issues in present day adoption. *Child Welfare, 63,* 233–243.

Duncan, G. J. & Hoffman, S. D. (1990). Teenage welfare receipt and subsequent dependence among black adolescent mothers. *Family Planning Perspectives, 22,* 16–20.

Dworkin, R. J., Harding, J. T., & Schreiber, N. B. (1993). Parenting or placing: Decision-making by pregnant teens. *Youth & Society, 25,* 75–92.

Edlin, S. (1954). *The unmarried mother in our society.* New York: Farrar, Straus and Young.

Edwards, D. S. (1995). Transformation of motherhood in adoption: The experiences of relinquishing mothers. Unpublished Ph.D. dissertation. University of North Florida: Jacksonville.

Edwards, D. S. (1999). The social control of illegitimacy through adoption. *Human Organization, 58*(4), 386–395.

Erikson, E. (1959). *Identity and the life cycle: Selected papers by Erik H. Erikson: Vol. I, Psychological issues.* New York: International Universities Press.

Erikson, E. (1968). *Identity: Youth and crisis.* New York: Norton.

Etter, J. (1993). Levels of cooperation and satisfaction in 56 open adoptions. *Child Welfare, 72,* 257–267.

Evan B. Donaldson Adoption Institute. (1997). *Benchmark adoption survey: Report on findings* (conducted by Princeton Survey Research Associates). New York: The Evan B. Donaldson Adoption Institute.

Evan B. Donaldson Adoption Institute. (1999a). *Openness in adoption and post-adoption contact agreements: A review of the empirical research and current state law.* New York: The Evan B. Donaldson Adoption Institute.

Evan B. Donaldson Adoption Institute (1999b). *Survey of adult Korean adoptees: Report on the findings.* New York: The Evan B. Donaldson Adoption Institute.

Fanshel, D. & Shinn, E. B. (1978). *Children in foster care.* New York: Columbia University Press.

Federal Register. (1998, September 18). [On-line]. Available: Federal Register Online via GPO Access, wais.access.gpo.gov. [DOCID:fr18se98-321].

Federal Register. (2000, January 25). Part II—Department of Health and Human Services, Administration for Children and Families, 45 CFR. Parts 1355, 1356, and 1357. Title IV-E Foster Care Eligibility Reviews and Child and Family Services State Plan Reviews; Final Rule. Washington, DC: Government Printing Office.

Festinger, T. B. (1971). Unwed mothers and their decisions to keep or surrender their children. *Child Welfare, 5,* 253–263.

Festinger, T. (1990). Adoption disruption: Rates and correlates. In D. M. Brodzinsky & M. D. Schechter (Eds.), *The psychology of adoption* (pp.201–218). New York: Oxford University Press.

Finley, G. E. (1999). Children of adoptive families. In W. K. Silverman & T. H. Ollendick (Eds.), *Developmental issues in clinical treatment of children* (pp. 359–370). Boston: Allyn and Bacon.

Fleming, T. (1956, March). The children we left behind. *Cosmopolitan*, Box 19, RG 319. Washington, DC: National Archives.

Fratter, J. (1991). Parties in the triangle. *Adoption and Fostering, 15*(4), 91–98.

Free, B. (1999). A history of adoption. *Adoption Network News, 12*(5), 6–8.

Freeman, M. & Freund, W. (1998). Working with adopted clients. *Journal of Analytic Social Work, 5*(4), 25–37.

Freivalds, S. (1999, Autumn). The Hague Convention on Intercountry Adoption. *The Bulletin,* 8–9.

Freundlich, M. (2000a). *The role of race, culture and national origin in adoption.* Washington, DC: CWLA Press.

Freundlich, M. (2000b). The market forces in adoption. Washington, DC: CWLA Press.

Freundlich, M. (1997). The future of adoption for children in foster care: Demographics in a changing socio-political environment. *Journal of Children and Poverty, 3*(2), 31–66.

Freundlich, M. (1999a, Winter). Clinical mediation. *Decree,* 3–5.

Freundlich, M. (1999b). Expediting termination of parental rights: Solving a problem or sowing the seeds of a new predicament? *Capital University Law Review, 28*(1), 97–110.

Freundlich, M. & Peterson, L. (1998). *Wrongful adoption: Law, policy and practice.* Washington, DC: Child Welfare League of America Press.

Frisk, M. (1964). Identity problems and confused conceptions of the genetic ego in adopted children during adolescence. *Acta Paedo Psychiatrica, 31,* 6–12.

Furstenberg, F., Jr., Brooks-Gunn, J., & Morgan, S. P. (1987). *Adolescent mothers in later life.* Cambridge, MA: Cambridge University Press.

Garrison, M. (1983). Why terminate parental rights. *Stanford Law Review, 35,* 423–437.

Geber, G. & Resnick, M. D. (1988). Family functioning of adolescents who parent and place for adoption. *Adolescence, 23*, 417–428.

Gelber, B. L. (1999). International adoption: Legal requirements and practical considerations. In J. H. Hollinger (Ed.), *Adoption law & practice, Vol. II* (pp. 11-1 through 11-29). New York: Matthew Bender & Co., Inc.

Gill, B. (in press). Adoption agencies and the search for the ideal family, 1918–1965. In E. W. Carp, (Ed.), *Adoption in history: New interpretative essays* (pp. 1–17). Lansing: University of Michigan Press.

Gill, C. (1991). Essay on the status of the American child, 2000 A.D.: Chattel or constitutionally protected child-citizen. *Ohio Northern Law Review, 17*, 543–567.

Gilles, T. & Kroll, J. (1991). *Barriers to same race placement.* St. Paul, MN: North American Council on Adoptable Children.

Gilligan, C. (1982). *In a different voice.* Cambridge, MA: Harvard University Press.

Gitlin, H. J. (1987). *Adoptions: An attorney's guide to helping adoptive parents.* Washington, DC: American Academy of Adoption Attorneys.

Goebels, B. & Lott, S. L. (1986, August 23). *Adoptees' resolution of the adolescent identity crisis: Where are the taproots?* Paper presented at the meeting of the American Psychological Association, Washington, DC.

Goodman, E. (1993, July 31). The biological parents won; the child lost. Jessica becomes Anna and that sends a message to adoptive parents. *The Philadelphia Inquirer*, p. A07.

Griswold v. Connecticut. (1965). 381 U.S. 479.

Gritter, J. L. (1997). *The spirit of open adoption.* Washington, DC: CWLA Press.

Gross, H. E. (1993). Open adoption: A research-based literature review and new data. *Child Welfare, 72*, 269–284.

Grotevant, H. D. (1997). Coming to terms with adoption: The construction of identity from adolescence into adulthood. *Adoption Quarterly, 1*, 3–27.

Grotevant, H. D. & McRoy, R. G. (1997). The Minnesota/Texas Adoption Research Project: Implications of openness in adoption for development and relationships. *Applied Developmental Science, 1*, 168–188.

Grotevant, H. D. & McRoy, R. G. (1998). *Openness in adoption: Exploring family connections.* Thousand Oaks, CA: Sage.

Grotevant, H. D., Ross, N. M., Marchel, M. A., & McRoy, R. G. (1999). Adaptive behavior in adopted children: Predictors from early risk, collaboration in relationships within the adoptive kinship network, and openness arrangements. *Journal of Adolescent Research, 14*(2), 231–247.

Groth, M. (1987). An agency moves toward open adoption of infants. *Child Welfare, 76*, 247–256.

Grow, L. J. (1979). Today's unmarried mothers: The choices have changed. *Child Welfare, 58*, 363–371.

Hacsi, T. (1995). From indenture to family foster care: A brief history of child placing. *Child Welfare, 74*, 162–180.

Hague Conference on Private International Law. (2000, February 15). Hague Convention of 29 May 1993 on Protection of Children and Co-operation in Respect of Intercountry Adoption. Status Sheet Convention #33. [On-line]. Available: http://hcch.net/e/status/adoshte.html

Haines, E. & Timms, N. (1985). *Adoption, identity, and social policy: The search for distant relatives.* Aldershot, England: Grower.

Hajal, F. & Rosenberg, E. B. (1991). The family life cycle in adoptive families. *American Journal of Orthopsychiatry, 61*, 78–85.

Hamilton, J. R. (1987/1988). The unwed father and the right to know of his child's existence. *Kentucky Law Journal, 76*, 949–1009.

Han, S. S. (1999). About Ae Ran Won. In S. Dorow (Ed.), *I wish for you a beautiful life: Letters from the Korean birth mothers of Ae Ran Won to their children* (pp. 132–134). St. Paul, MN: Yeong and Yeong Book Company.

Harris, F. & Whyte, N. (1999). Support for birth mothers in a group setting. *Adoption & Fostering, 23*(4), 41–48.

Hartman, A. & Laird, J. (1990). Family treatment after adoption: Common themes. In D. Brodzinsky & M. D. Schechter (Eds.), *The psychology of adoption* (pp. 221–239). New York/Oxford: Oxford University Press.

Hirst, J. (1997, January). Adopting a stance. *Community Care, 23*, 11–12.

Hodges, J. & Tizard, B. (1989). IQ and behavioral adjustment of ex-institutional adolescents. *Journal of Psychiatry, 30*, 53–75.

Hofferth, S. L. (1987). Social and economic consequences of teenage childbearing. In S. L. Hofferth & C. D. Hayes (Eds.), *Risking the future: Adolescent sexuality, pregnancy and childbearing, Vol.2* (pp. 123–144). Washington, DC: National Academy Press.

Hoffman-Riem, C. (1990). *The adopted child: Family life with double parenthood.* New Jersey: Transaction Publishers.

Hoffman-Riem, C. (1989, May/June). Disclosing adoption. *Society*, 26–31.

Holden, N. L. (1991). Adoption and eating disorders: A high-risk group? *British Journal of Psychiatry, 158*, 829–833.

Hollinger, J. H. (1995). Adoption and aspiration: The Uniform Adoption Act, the DeBoer-Schmidt case, and the American quest for the ideal family. *Duke Journal of Gender Law & Policy, 2*(1), 15–40.

Hollinger, J. H. (1996). The Uniform Adoption Act: Reporter's ruminations. *Family Law Quarterly, 30*(2), 345–378.

Hollinger, J. H. (1998, November 5). *Openness and adoptive family autonomy: Implications for adoption law & practice.* Presentation at the Conference of the Association of Administrators of the Interstate Compact on Adoption and Medical Assistance, Oklahoma City, OK.

Hollinger, J. H. (1999a). Aftermath of adoption: Legal and social consequences. In J. H. Hollinger (Ed.), *Adoption law & practice: Volume II* (pp. 13-1 through 13-113). New York: Matthew Bender & Co., Inc.

Hollinger, J. H. (1999b). Consent to adoption. In J. H. Hollinger (Ed.), *Adoption law & practice, Volume I* (pp. 2-1 through 2-130). New York: Matthew Bender & Co., Inc.

Hollinger, J. H. (in press). Authenticity and identity in contemporary adoptive families. *Journal of Gender Specific Medicine.*

Holt Children's Services. (1999). Status of adoption (1955–1998). South Korea: Holt International Children's Services.

Hoopes, J. L. (1990). Adoption and identity formation. In D. Brodzinsky & M. Schechter (Eds.), *The psychology of adoption* (pp. 144–166). New York: Oxford University Press.

Howe, M. B. (1999). Helping a birth mother heal. In C. Marshner & W. L. Pierce (Eds.), *Adoption Factbook III* (pp. 338–340). Washington, DC: National Council for Adoption.

Hughes, B. (1995). Openness and contact in adoption: A child-centered perspective. *British Journal of Social Work, 25,* 729–747.

Hughes, B. & Logan, J. (1993). *Birth parents: The hidden dimension.* Manchester, England: University of Manchester, Department of Social Policy and Social Work.

Human Rights Watch. (1998). *Abandoned to the state: Cruelty and neglect in Russian orphanages.* New York: Human Rights Watch.

Humphrey, M. (1986). Infertility as a marital crisis. *Stress Management, 2,* 221–224.

In re Adoption of Doe. (1994). 638 N.E.2d 181 Illinois. Sub nom In re Petition of Kirchner. (1995). 649 N.E.2d 324 (Illinois).

In re Baby Girl Clausen. (1993). 502 W. N.W.2d 649 (Michigan).

Inglis, K. (1984). *Living mistakes: Mothers who consented to adoption.* Sydney, Australia: Allen Unwin.

International News Service. (1956, June 6). Expiration of Refugee Act will affect orphans here. *Nippon Times,* p. 5.

Jacokes, L. (1965). MMPI Prediction of the unwed mother's decision regarding child placement. *Journal of Clinical Psychology, 21,* 103–109.

Jane Does 1, 2, 3, 4 v. the State of Oregon, John A. Kitzhaber, and Edward Johnson. (1999). 164 Or. App. 543, 993 P.2d 822.

Johnson, K., Banghan, H., & Liyao, W. (1998). Infant abandonment and adoption in China. *Population and Development Review, 24,* 469–510.

Kadushin, A. (1970). Adoptive status: Birth parents vs. bread parents. *Child Care Quarterly Review, 24,* 10–14.

Kadushin, A. (1980). *Child welfare services* (3rd ed.). New York: Macmillan.

Kalmuss, D. (1992). Adoption and black teenagers: The viability of a pregnancy resolution strategy. *Journal of Marriage and the Family, 54,* 485–495.

Kanuik, J. (1994). Strategies in recruiting black adopters. *Adoption & Fostering, 15*(1), 38–41.

Katz, M. (1986). *In the shadow of the poorhouse: A social history of welfare in America.* NY: Basic Books.

Kaye, K. (1990). Acknowledgment or rejection of differences? In D. Brodzinsky & M. Schechter (Eds.), *The psychology of adoption* (pp. 121–143). New York: Oxford University Press.

Kennedy, R. (1994). Orphans of separatism: The painful politics of transracial adoption. *The American Prospect, 17*, 38–45.

Kirk, H. D. (1985). *Adoptive kinship: A modern institution in need of reform* (Rev. ed.). Port Angeles, WA: Ben-Simon Publications.

Kirk, H. D. (1984). *Shared fate: A theory and method of adoptive relationships.* New York: The Free Press.

Kirschner, D. H. (1992). Understanding adoptees who kill: Dissociation, patricide, and the psychodynamics of adoption. *International Journal of Offender Therapy and Comparative Criminology, 36*, 323–33.

Kirschner, D. H. & Nagel, L. (1988). Antisocial behavior in adoptees: Patterns and dynamics. *Child and Adolescent Social Work, 5*, 300–314.

Kligman, G. (1992, June 1). Abortion and international adoption in post-Ceausescu Romania. *Feminist Studies, 18*, 405.

Kolata, G. (1999, March 3). $50,000 offered to tall, smart egg donor. *The New York Times*, p. A10.

Kowal, K. A. & Schilling, K. M. (1985). Adoption through the eyes of adult adoptees. *American Journal of Orthopsychiatry, 55*, 354–362.

Langsam, M. (1964). *Children west: A history of the placing-out system of the NY Children's Aid Society.* Madison, WI: The Department of History, University of Wisconsin.

Lawton, J. & Gross, S. (1964). Review of the psychiatric literature on adopted children. *Archives of General Psychiatry, 11*, 663–694.

Lehmann, D. J. (1999, March 17). Baby T ruling gets attention. *Chicago Sun Times.* Available: www.suntimes.com:80/output/news/fed17i.html.

Lehr v. Robinson. (1983). 463 U.S. 248.

Levy-Shiff, R., Bar, O., & Har-Even, D. (1990). Psychological adjustment of adoptive parents-to-be. *American Journal of Orthopsychiatry, 60*, 258–267.

Leynes, C. (1980). Keep or adopt: A study of factors influencing pregnant adolescents' plans for their babies. *Child Psychiatry and Human Development, 11*(2), 105–113.

Lieberman, E. J. (1998). Adoption and identity. *Adoption Quarterly,* *2*(2), 1–5.

Lifton, B. J. (1988). *Lost and found: The adoption experience.* New York: Harper & Row.

Lifton, B. J. (1994). *Journey of the adopted self: A quest for wholeness.* New York: Basic Books.

Lightman, E. & Schlesinger, B. (1982). Pregnant adolescents in maternity homes: Some professional concerns. In R. R. Stuart & C. F. Wells (Eds.), *Pregnancy in adolescence: Needs, problems, and management* (pp. 363–406). New York: Van Nostrand Reinhold Company.

Lipman, E. L., Offord, D. R., Boyle, M. H., & Racine, Y.A. (1993). Follow-up of psychiatric and educational morbidity among adopted children. *Journal of the American Academy of Child and Adolescent Psychiatry, 32,* 1007–1012.

Littell, J. H. (1997). Effects of the duration, intensity and breadth of family preservation services: A new analysis of data from the Illinois Family First experiment. *Children and Youth Services Review, 19,* 17–39.

Littlewood, T. B. (1977). *The politics of population control.* Notre Dame, IN: University of Notre Dame Press.

Littner, N. (1975). The importance of the natural parents to the child in placement. *Child Welfare, 54,* 175–181.

Lowe, H. (1999). A birthmother's view of adoption. *Roots and Wings, 42,* 31–33.

Lücker-Babel, M. F. (1990). *Intercountry adoption and trafficking in children: An initial assessment of the adequacy of the international protection of children and their rights.* Geneva, Switzerland: Defence for Children International.

M.L.B. v. S.L.J. (1996). 519 U.S. 102.

MacFadyen, S. (1995). 'Preparing' or 'deterring?' Consumer feedback on preparation groups for prospective adoptive parents in Barnardo's Family Placement Project, Edinburgh. In R. Fuller & A. Petch (Eds.), *Practitioner research: The reflexive social worker* (pp. 140–150). Buckingham, England: Open University Press.

McHutchinson, J. (1986). *Relinquishing a child: The circumstances and effects of loss.* Unpublished paper. On file at the University of New South Wales, Australia.

McKenna, M. (1989). *What makes a good adoptive parent?* Unpublished Master of Science dissertation, University of Stirling, Scotland.

McLaughlin, S., Manninen, D. L., & Winges, L. D. (1988a). Do adolescents who relinquish their children fare better or worse than those who raise them? *Family Planning Perspectives, 20,* 25–32.

McLaughlin, S., Manninen, D. L., & Winges, L. D. (1988b). The consequences of the relinquishment decision among adolescent mothers. *Social Work, 33,* 320–324.

McRoy, R. G. (1999). *Special needs adoption: Practice issues.* New York: Garland Publishing, Inc.

McRoy, R. G. & Grotevant, H. D. (1988a). Open adoptions: Practice and policy issues. *Journal of Social Work and Human Sexuality, 6,* 119–132.

McRoy, R. G., Grotevant, H. D. & Zurcher, L. A. (1988b). *The development of emotional disturbance in adopted adolescents: Origins and development.* New York: Praeger.

McRoy, R. G. & Zurcher, L. A. (1983). *Transracial and inracial adoptees: The adolescent years.* Springfield, IL: Charles C. Thomas.

McWhinnie, A. M. (1969). The adopted child in adolescence. In G. Caplan & S. Lebovice (Eds.), *Adolescence* (pp. 122–143). New York: Basic Books.

McWhinnie, A. M. (1994). The concept of open adoption: How valid is it. In A. McWhinnie & J. Smith (Eds.), *Current human dilemmas in adoption* (pp. 112–132). Dundee, Scotland: University of Dundee.

Maine Task Force on Adoption. (1989). *Adoption: A life long process.* Portland, ME: Maine Department of Human Resources.

Mann, S. (1998). Adoptive parents: A practice perspective. *Adoption & Fostering, 22*(3), 42–51.

Marcia, J. (1980). Identity in adolescent. In J. Adelson (Ed.), *Handbook of adolescence psychology* (pp. 46–77). New York: Wiley.

Marquis, K. S. & Detweiler, R. A. (1985). Does adoption mean different? An attributional analysis. *Journal of Personality and Social Psychology, 48*, 1054–1066.

Martin, C. (1988). *Beating the adoption game.* New York: Harcourt Brace Jovanovich.

Martin, P. (1999, July 13) Hammurabi's Code of Laws. The Code of Laws 151-200. [On-line] Available: http://members.xoom.com/_XOOM/PMartin/hammurabi_law151-200.htm

Mason, M. M. (1995a). *Out of the shadows: Birthfathers' stories.* Edina, MN: O.J. Howard Publishing.

Mason, M. M. (1995b, October, November, December). Bringing birthfathers into the adoption loop. *Roots & Wings,* 27–30.

Mason, K. & Selman, P. (1997). Birth parents' experiences of contested adoption. *Adoption & Fostering, 21*(1), 21–28.

May, E. T. (1988). *Homeward bound: American families in the cold war era.* New York: Basic Books.

Mech, E. V. (1986). Pregnant adolescents: Communicating the adoption option. *Child Welfare, 65*, 555–567.

Medora, N. P., Goldstein, A., & von der Heller, C. (1993). Variables related to romanticism and self-esteem in pregnant teenagers. *Adolescence, 28*(109), 159–170.

Melina, L. & Roszia, S. K. (1993). *The open adoption experience.* New York: Harper Collins.

Menard, B. J. (1997). A birth father and adoption in the perinatal setting. In R. F. Lind & D. H. Bachman (Ed.), *Fundamentals of perinatal social work: A guide for clinical practice* (pp. 153–163). Binghamton, NY: Haworth Press.

Meyer, H. J., Borgatta, E. F., & Fanshel, D. (1959). Unwed mothers' decisions about their babies: An interim replication study. *Child Welfare, 38*, 5–6.

Meyer v. Nebraska. (1923). 262 U.S. 390.

Miall, C. (1987). The stigma of adoptive parent status: Perceptions of community attitudes toward adoption and the experience of informal social sanctioning. *Journal of Applied Family and Child Studies, 36*, 34–39.

Mikawa, J. K. & Boston, J. A. (1968). Psychological characteristics of adopted children. *Psychiatric Quarterly Supplement, 42*, 274–281.

Modell, J. S. (1994). *Kinship with strangers: Adoption and interpretations of kinship in American culture.* Berkeley: University of California Press.

Moore, J. & Fombonne, E. (1999). Psychopathology in adopted and nonadopted children: A clinical sample. *American Journal of Orthopsychiatry, 69*(3), 403–409.

Mott, F. & Marsiglio, W. (1985). Early childbearing and completion of high school. *Family Planning Perspectives, 17,* 234–237.

Munson, W. (1993). *All talk: The talkshow in media culture.* Philadelphia: Temple University Press.

Musick, J. S., Handler, A., & Waddill, K. D. (1984). Teens and adoption: A pregnancy resolution alternative? *Children Today,* 24–29.

Namerow, P. B., Kalmuss, D. S., & Cushman, L. F. (1993). The determinants of young women's pregnancy-resolution choices. *Journal of Research on Adolescence, 3,* 193–215.

National Committee for Adoption (1989). *1989 Adoption Factbook: United States data, issues, regulations and resources.* Washington, DC: National Committee for Adoption.

National Council for Adoption. (1997a). Who stands for adoption? *National Adoption Reports, 18*(2), 1–2.

National Council for Adoption. (1997b). Brief of Appellants, *Doe v. Sunquist,* No. 96-6197, 1997 Fed. App. 0051P (6th Cir.).

National Council for Adoption. (1999). *Adoption Factbook III.* Washington, DC: National Council for Adoption.

National Urban League. (1960, September 16). *The current attack on ADC in Louisiana.* Florence Crittenton Association of America Papers. Minneapolis: Social Welfare History Archives, University of Minnesota.

Nelson, K. A. (1985). *On the frontier of adoption: A study of special needs adoptive families.* New York: Child Welfare League of America.

Neubauer, R. (1988). Babies for sale. *World Press Review, 35*(8), 57.

Nickman, S. L. (1985). Losses in adoption: The need for dialogue. *Psychoanalytic Study of the Child, 40,* 365–398.

Norvell, M. & Guy, R. F. (1977). A comparison of self-concept in adopted and nonadopted adolescents. *Adolescence, 12,* 274–448.

O'Neill, T. (1994, September/October). Birthfather rights. *Adoptive Families,* 8–12.

O'Shaughnessy, T. (1994). *Adoption, social work, and social theory: Making the connections.* Avebury, England: Ashgate Publishing Limited.

Partridge, P. (1991). The particular challenges of being adopted. *Smith College Studies in Social Work, 61*(2), 197–208.

Pastor, R. (1989, May). The Honduran baby market. *Sojourner: The Women's Forum,* 19.

Paton, J. M. (1954). *The adopted break silence: The experiences and views of forty adults who were adopted as children.* Philadelphia: Life History Center.

Paulson, J. O., Haarmann, B. S., Salerno, R. L., & Asmar, P. (1988). An investigation of the relationship between emotional maladjustment and infertility. *Fertility and Sterility, 49,* 258–262.

Pavao, J. M. (1998). *The family of adoption.* Boston: Beacon Press.

Perry, T. L. (1998). Transracial and international adoption: Mothers, hierarchy, race and feminist legal theory. *Yale Journal of Law and Feminism, 10,* 101–164.

Phillips, R. (1998). Disabled children in permanent substitute families. In C. Robinson & K. Stalker (Eds.), *Growing up with disability* (pp. 155–175). London: Jessica Kingsley Publishers.

Pierce, W. (1997, February 11). *On-Line Forum: Opening adoption records.* [On-line]. Available: http://www1.pbs.org/newshour/forum/february97/adoption.html

Pierce, W. L. (1999a). Open adoption. In C. Marshner & W. L. Pierce (Eds.), *Adoption Factbook III* (pp. 233–238). Washington, DC: The National Council for Adoption.

Pierce, W. L. (1999b). Twenty-one barriers to adoption. In C. Marshner & W. L. Pierce (Eds.), *Adoption Factbook III* (pp. 556–587). Washington, DC: National Council for Adoption.

Pilotti, F. J. (1985) Intercountry adoption: A view from Latin America. *Child Welfare, 64,* 25–35.

Pilotti, F. J. (1993). Intercountry adoption: Trends, issues and policy implications for the 1990s. In *Childhood: Vol. I* (pp. 165–177). Montevideo, Uruguay: Instituto Interamericano del Niño.

Planned Parenthood v. Casey. (1992). 505 U.S. 833.

Plomin, R. & DeFries, J. C. (1985). *Origins of individual differences in infancy: The Colorado Adoption Project.* New York: Academic Press.

Prager, D. (1999). Men and adoption: Do you love your child or your seed? In C. Marshner & W. L. Pierce (Eds.), *Adoption Factbook III* (pp. 362–364). Washington, DC: National Council for Adoption.

Pugh, G. & Schofield, G. (1999). Unlocking the past: The experience of gaining access to Barnardo's records. *Adoption & Fostering, 23*(2), 7–18.

Quillion v. Walcott. (1978). 434 U.S. 246.

Reitz, M. & Watson, K. W. (1992). *Adoption and the family system.* New York: Guilford Press.

Resnick, M. D. (1984). Studying adolescent mothers' decision making about adoption and parenting. *Social Work, 29,* 5–10.

Resnick, M. D., Blum, R. W., Bose, J., Smith, M., & Toogood, R. (1990). Characteristics of unmarried adolescent mothers: Determinants of child rearing versus adoption. *American Journal of Orthopsychiatry, 60,* 577–584.

Reynolds, W. F., Eisnitz, M. F., Chiappise, D., & Walsh, M. (1976, September 4). *Personality factors differentiating searching and non-searching adoptees.* Paper presented at the 84th Annual Convention of the American Psychological Association, Washington, DC.

Rickarby, G. A. & Egan, P. (1980). Issues of preventive work with adopted adolescents. *Medical Journal of Australia, 1,* 470–472.

Ripple, L. (1953). *Social work standards of unmarried parenthood as affected by contemporary treatment formulations.* Unpublished doctoral dissertation, University of Chicago.

Roberts v. United States Jaycees. (1984). 468 U.S. 609.

Rogeness, G. A., Hoppe, S. K., Macedo, C. A., Fischer, C., & Harris, W. R. (1988). Psychopathology in hospitalized adopted children. *Journal of the American Academy of Child and Adolescent Psychiatry, 27,* 628–631.

Rohner, R. P. (1986). *The warmth dimension: Foundations of parental acceptance-rejection theory.* Beverly Hills, CA: Sage.

Romanchik, B. (1996, Summer). The benefits of open adoption. *Open Adoption: Birthparent, 9,* 1,7.

Romanchik, B. (1997a, Winter). Parenting after relinquishment: Part I. *Open Adoption: Birthparent, 11,* 1,4.

Romanchik, B. (1997b, Summer). Birthparent transformation: Defining our public and self images. *Open Adoption: Birthparent, 13,* 1–2.

Romanchik, B. (1999). *What is open adoption?* Royal Oak, MI: R-Squared Press.

Roots and Wings. (1996). Casting the "Net" for answers. *Roots and Wings, 8*(1), 28–29.

Rosenberg, E. B. (1992). *The adoption life cycle: The children and their families through the years.* New York: Free Press.

Rosenberg, E. B. & Horner, T. M. (1991). Birth parent romances and identity formation in adopted children. *American Journal of Orthopsychiatry, 61,* 70–77.

Rotundo, E. A. (1985). American fatherhood: A historical perspective. *American Behavioral Scientist, 29,* 7–24.

Rushton, A., Quinton, D., & Treseder, J. (1993). New parents for older children: Support services during eight years of placement. *Adoption & Fostering, 17*(4), 39–45.

Ryburn, M. (1991). The myth of assessment. *Adoption & Fostering, 15*(1), 21–27.

Ryburn, M. (1992). Contested adoption proceedings. *Adoption & Fostering, 16*(4), 29–38.

Ryburn, M. (1995). Adopted children's identity and information needs. *Children and Society, 9*(3), 41–64.

Rycus, J. S., Hughes, R. C., & Goodman, D. A. (1998). Adoption. In J. S. Rycus & R. C. Hughes (Eds.), *Field Guide To Child Welfare: Vol. 4* (pp. 881–1038). Washington, DC: CWLA Press.

Sabalis, R. F. & Burch, E. A. (1980). Comparisons of psychiatric problems of adopted and non-adopted patients. *Southern Medical Journal, 73,* 867–868.

Sachdev, P. (1991). Achieving openness in adoption: Some critical issues in policy formulation. *American Journal of Orthopsychiatry, 61(2),* 241–249.

Sandelowski, M. (1995). A theory of the transition to parenthood of infertile couples. *Research in Nursing & Health, 18,* 123–132.

Sants, H. J. (1964). Genealogical bewilderment in children with substitute parents. *British Journal of Medical Psychology, 37,* 133–141.

Saunders, B. (1996, Spring). Birthfathers come of age. *Birthparent, 8,* 1.

Scarnecchia, S. (1995). A child's right to protection from transfer trauma in a contested adoption case. *Duke Journal of Gender Law and Policy, 2,* 41–63.

Schaefer, C. (1991). *The other mother.* New York: Soho Press.

Schechter, M. (1960). Observations on adopted children. *Archives of General Psychiatry, 3,* 21–32.

Schechter, M. & Bertocci, D. (1990). The meaning of search. In D. Brodzinsky & M. Schechter (Eds.), *The psychology of adoption* (pp. 62–92). New York/Oxford: Oxford University Press.

Schechter, M. D., Carlson, P., Simmons, J. & Work, H. (1964). Emotional problems in the adoptee. *Archives in General Psychiatry, 10,* 37–46.

Schoenberg, C. (1974). On adoption and identity. *Child Welfare, 53,* 549.

Schwartz, L. L. (1986). Unwed fathers and adoption custody disputes. *American Journal of Family Therapy, 14*(4), 347–355.

Sellick, C. & Thoburn, J. (1996). *What works in family placement?* Essex, England: Barnardos.

Shapiro, C. H. (1993). *When part of the self is lost: Helping clients heal after sexual and reproductive losses.* San Francisco: Jossey-Bass.

Sharma, A. R., McGue, M. K., & Benson, P. L. (1996a). The emotional and behavioral adjustment of United States adopted adolescents. Part I: A comparison study. *Children and Youth Services Review, 18,* 77–94.

Sharma, A. R., McGue, M. K., & Benson, P. L. (1996b). The emotional and behavioral adjustment of United States adopted adolescents. Part II: Age at adoption. *Children and Youth Services Review, 18,* 95–108.

Sharma, A. R., McGue, M. K., & Benson, P. L. (1998). The psychological adjustment of United States adopted adolescents and their nonadopted siblings. *Child Development, 69*(3), 791–802.

Sherman, J. M. (1989). *Identifying parents who request foster care: An epidemiological survey.* Masters thesis, Southern Connecticut State University. UMI #1339859.

Siegel, D. H. (1993). Open adoption of infants: Adoptive parents' perceptions of advantages and disadvantages. *Social Work, 38,* 15–23.

Silber, K. & Dorner, P. M. (1990). *Children of open adoption.* San Antonio, TX: Corona.

Silver, L. B. (1970). Frequency of adoption in children with neurological learning disability syndrome. *Journal of Learning Disabilities, 3,* 10–14.

Silver, L. B. (1989). Frequency of adoption of children and adolescents with learning disabilities. *Journal of Learning Disabilities, 22,* 325–328.

Silverman, P. R. (1981). *Helping women cope with grief.* Newbury Park, NY: Sage Publications.

Silverstein, D. R. & Demick, J. (1994). Toward an organizational-relational model of open adoption. *Family Process, 33,* 111–124.

Silverstein, D. R. & Roszia, S. K. (1999). Openness: A critical component of special needs adoption. *Child Welfare, 78,* 637–651.

Simon, N. M. & Senturia, A. G. (1966). Adoption and psychiatric illness. *American Journal of Psychiatry, 122,* 858–867.

Singer, I. M., Brodzinsky, D. M., Ramsey, D. R., Steir, M., & Waters, E. (1985). Mother-infant attachment in adoptive families. *Child Development, 56,* 1543–1551.

Small, J. W. (1987). Working with adoptive families. *Public Welfare, 45*(3), 33–41.

Smith, S. L. & Howard, J. A. (1994). *The Adoption Preservation Project 30.* Normal: Illinois State University Department of Social Work.

Smith, J. & Miroff, F. I. (1987). *You're our child: The adoption experience.* New York: Madison Books.

Smothers, R. (1997, December 18). Accord lets gay couples adopt jointly. *The New York Times,* p. B4.

Sobol, M. P. & Cardiff, J. (1983). A sociopsychological investigation of adult adoptees' search for birth parents. *Family Relations, 32,* 477–483.

Sokoloff, B. Z. (1993). Antecedents of American adoption. *The Future of Children, 3*(1), 17–25.

Solinger, R. (1992). *Wake up little Susie: Single pregnancy and race before* Roe v. Wade. New York: Routledge.

Sorosky, A. D., Baran, A., & Pannor, R. (1975). Identity conflicts in adoptees. *American Journal of Orthopsychiatry, 45,* 18–27.

Sorosky, A. D., Baran, A., & Pannor, R. (1984). *The adoption triangle.* Garden City, NY: Anchor Books.

Spencer, M. (1999). Adoption vocabulary. In C. Marshner & W. L. Pierce (Eds.), *Adoption Factbook III* (pp. 12–17). Washington, D.C.: National Council for Adoption.

Stanley v. Illinois (1972). 405 U.S. 645.

Stein, L. M. & Hoopes, J. L. (1985). *Identity formation in the adopted adolescent.* New York: Child Welfare League of America.

Stevenson, P. (1991). A model of self-assessment for prospective adopters. *Adoption & Fostering, 15*(3), 30–34.

Stolley, K. (1993). Statistics on adoption in the United States. *The Future of Children: Adoption, 3*(1), 26–42.

Strobino, D. M. (1987). The health and medical consequences of adolescent sexuality and pregnancy: A review of the literature. In S. L. Hoffert & C. D. Hayes (Eds.), *Risking the future: Adolescent sexuality, pregnancy and childbearing, Vol. 2* (pp. 93–122). Washington, DC: National Academy Press.

Styles, M. B. (1999). Counseling birth mothers. In C. Marshner & W. L. Pierce (Eds.), *Adoption Factbook III* (pp. 308–313). Washington, DC: National Council for Adoption.

Tatara, T. (1993). *Characteristics of Children in Substitutive and Adoptive Care.* Washington, D.C.: The Voluntary Cooperative Information System, The American Public Welfare Association.

Thompson, K. G., Hollinger, J. H., & Dorff, V. (1999). Contested adoptions: Strategy of the case. In J. H. Hollinger (Ed.), *Adoption law & practice, Vol. 2* (pp. 8-1 through 8-109). New York: Matthew Bender & Co., Inc.

Thompson, L. A. & Plomin, R. (1988). The sequenced inventory of communication development: An adoption study of two- and three-year olds. *International Journal of Behavioral Development, 11,* 219–231.

Tienari, P., Lahti, I., Sorri, A., Naarala, M., Moring, J., Kaleva, M., Wahlberg, K., & Wynne, L. C. (1990). Adopted-away offspring of schizophrenics and controls: The Finnish adoptive family study of schizophrenia. In L. Robins & M. Rutter (Eds.), *Straight and deviant pathways from childhood to adulthood* (pp. 365–379). New York: Cambridge University Press.

Triseliotis, J. (1973). *In search of origins: The experience of adopted people.* London: Routledge & Kegan Paul.

Triseliotis, J. (1984). Obtaining birth certificates. In P. Bean (Ed.), *Adoption: Essays in social policy, law and sociology* (pp. 110–126). London: Tavistock.

Triseliotis, J. (1993). Open adoption: The evidence examined. In M. Adcock, M. Kaniuk, & J. White (Eds), *Exploring openness in adoption* (pp. 33–60). London: Batsford/BAAF.

Triseliotis, J. & Hill, M. (1990). Contrasting adoption, foster care, and residential rearing. In D. M. Brodzinsky & M. D. Schechter (Eds.),

The psychology of adoption (pp. 107–120). New York: Oxford University Press.

UNICEF. (2000, November 8). Intercountry adoption: Information portfolio—Guatemala. [On-line]. Available: http://www.unicef-icdc.it/information/portfolios/intercountry-adoption/current/index.htm.

Uniform Adoption Act. (1998). In J. H. Hollinger (Ed.), *Adoption law & practice* (Appendix 4-A). New York: Matthew Bender & Co., Inc.

U.S. Children's Bureau. (1938, July). Legislation and regulations relating to separation of babies from their mother. *The Child, 3*, 19–21.

United States Department of State (Reported by Holt International Children's Service). (2000, January). International adoption statistics: Top twenty source countries for adoptions FY 1999. [On-line]. Available: http://www.holtintl.org/ins1999.html.

Utah Code Annotated. (1996). Sections 78-30-4.12(2), 78-30-4.13(I).

Van Keppel, M. & Winkler, R. (1983, April 23). The adjustment of relinquishing mothers in adoption: The results of a national study. Presented to the First NSCMC and ARMS conference, Melbourne, Australia.

Veevers, H. M. (1991). Which child: Which family? *Transactional Analysis Journal, 21*(4), 207–211.

Veevers, J. (1980). *Childless by choice.* Toronto: Butterworths.

Verhovek, S. H. (1997, November 30). Homosexual foster parent sets off a debate in Texas. *The New York Times*, p. 20.

Verhulst, F. C., Althaus, M. S., & Versluis-den Bieman, H. J. M. (1990a). Problem behavior in international adoptees: I. An epidemiological study. *Journal of the American Academy of Child and Adolescent Psychiatry, 29*, 94–103.

Verhulst, F. C., Althaus, M., & Versluis-den Bieman, H. J. M. (1990b). Problem behavior in international adoptees: II. Age at placement. *Journal of the American Academy of Child and Adolescent Psychiatry, 31*, 518–524.

Verhulst, F. C. & Versluis-den Bieman, H. J. M. (1992). Damaging backgrounds: Later adjustment of international adoptees. *Journal of the American Academy of Child and Adolescent Psychiatry, 31*, 518–524.

Verhulst, F. C. & Versluis-den Bieman, H. J. M. (1995). Developmental course of problem behaviors in adolescent adoptees. *Journal of* the American Academy of Child and Adolescent Psychiatry, 34, 151–158.

Verrier, N. (1993). *The primal wound.* Baltimore: Gateway Press.

Waggenspack, B. M. (1998). The symbolic crises of adoption: Popular media's agenda setting. *Adoption Quarterly, 1*(4), 57–82.

Walby, C. & Symons, B. (1990). *Who am I? Identity, adoption and human fertilisation.* London: British Association of Adoption and Fostering.

Wald, M. (1976). State intervention on behalf of "neglected" children: Standards for removal of children from their homes, monitoring the status of children in foster care, and termination of parental rights. *Stanford Law Review, 28,* 625–706.

Ward, M. (1998). The impact of adoption on the new parents' marriage. *Adoption Quarterly, 2*(2), 57–78.

Warren, S. B. (1992). Lower threshold for referral for psychiatric treatment for adopted adolescents. *Journal of the American Academy of Child and Adolescent Psychiatry, 31,* 512–517.

Watson, K. (1988, Fall). The case for open adoption. *Public Welfare,* 24–28.

Watson, K. (1994). Should adoption records be opened? Yes. In E. Gambrill & T. J. Stein (Eds.), *Controversial issues in child welfare* (pp. 223–229). Boston: Allyn and Bacon.

Wegar, K. (1997). *Adoption, identity, and kinship: The debate over sealed birth records.* New Haven: Yale University Press.

Weinman, M. L., Robinson, M., Simmons, J. T., Schreiber, N. B., & Stafford, B. (1989). Pregnant teens: Differential pregnancy resolution and treatment implications. *Child Welfare, 67*(1), 45–55.

Weintraub, M. & Konstam, V. (1995). Birthmothers: Silent relationships. *Affilia, 10*(3), 315–327.

Wells, S. (1993). Post-traumatic stress disorder in birth mothers. *Adoption & Fostering, 17*(4), 22–26.

Wendell, M. & Rosenbaum, B. R. (1999). Interstate adoptions: Interstate compact on the placement of children. In J. H. Hollinger (Ed.), *Adoption Law & Practice, Vol. I* (pp. 3A-1 through 3A-33). New York: Matthew Bender & Co., Inc.

Wieder, H. (1978). On when and whether to disclose about adoption. *Journal of the American Psychoanalytic Association, 26,* 793–811.

Winkler, R. & Van Keppel, M. (1984). *Relinquishing mothers in adoption: Their long term adjustment* (Monograph #3). Melbourne, Australia: Institute of Family Studies.

Winkler, R. C., Brown, D. W., Van Keppel, M., & Blanchard, A. (1988). *Clinical practice in adoption.* New York: Pergamon Press.

Winter, C. (1997, December 16). The biological imperative (Part 2 of The Fertility Race). *MSNBC.* [On-line]. Available: http://www.msnbc.com/news/130623.asp

Wisconsin v. Yoder. (1972). 406 U.S. 205.

Woodhouse, M. (1994). "Out of children's needs, children's rights": The child's voice in defining the family. *Brigham Young University Journal of Public Law, 8*(2), 321.

Wright, J., Bissonnette, F., Duchesne, C., Benoit, J., Sabovrin, S., & Girard, Y. (1991). Psychological distress and infertility: Men and women respond differently. *Fertility and Sterility, 55,* 100–108.

Wulczyn, F. (1991). *The community dimension of permanency planning.* New York: New York State Department of Social Services, Division of Family and Children Services.

Yngvesson, B. (1997). Negotiating motherhood: Identity and differences in "open" adoptions. *Law & Society Review, 31*(1), 31–80.

Zacharias, Y. (2000, January 18). Adoptive parents must hand over baby to birth father. *The Vancouver Sun.* Available: http://national post. Com/news.asp?f=000118/179832

Zelizer, V. (1985). *Pricing the priceless child.* Princeton, NJ: Princeton University Press.

About the Authors

Madelyn Freundlich is policy director for Children's Rights, Inc., New York, NY. She formerly served as the executive director of the Evan B. Donaldson Adoption Institute and as general counsel for the Child Welfare League of America. She is a social worker and lawyer whose worked has focused on child welfare policy and practice for the past decade. She has authored a number of books and articles on child welfare law and policy. Her most recent writing has focused on the impact of welfare reform on foster care and special needs adoption; the role of race and culture in adoption; interstate adoption law and practice; genetic testing in adoption evaluations; and confidentiality in child welfare practice. Ms. Freundlich holds masters degrees in social work and public health and holds a JD and LL.M.

Joy Kim Lieberthal is the adoption program manager at the Adoption Education Institute and Adoptive Family Magazine. Formally, she was a Policy Analyst at the Evan B. Donaldson Adoption Institute. She received her masters degree in social work from Columbia University. She is also a board member and mentorship director of Also-Known-As, Inc. Joy has spoken on a number of panels to adoption professionals, adoptive families, and has done extensive work with adopted children and teens. She has presented on issues related to international adoption and ethical issues in adoption at various national conferences. She has written for transcultured magazine and is recently published in *Voices from Another Place: An Anthology.*